THE AUSTRALIAN
Women's Weekly

QUICK & EASY

THE AUSTRALIAN **Women's Weekly**

QUICK & EASY

SIMPLE, EVERYDAY RECIPES IN 30 MINUTES OR LESS

Project Editor Siobhán O'Connor
Project Designer Alison Shackleton
Editors Kiron Gill, Megan Lea
Jacket Designer Alison Donovan
Jackets Coordinator Jasmin Lennie
Production Editor David Almond
Production Controller Denitsa Kenanska
Managing Editor Dawn Henderson
Managing Art Editor Alison Donovan
Art Director Maxine Pedliham
Publishing Director Katie Cowan

First published in Great Britain in 2022
by Dorling Kindersley Limited
DK, One Embassy Gardens, 8 Viaduct Gardens, London, SW11 7BW

The authorized representative in the EEA is Dorling Kindersley
Verlag GmbH. Arnulfstr. 124, 80636 Munich, Germany

Copyright © 2022 Dorling Kindersley Limited
A Penguin Random House Company
10 9 8 7 6 5 4 3 2 1
001–326302–Mar/2022

A CIP catalogue record for this book is available from the British Library.
ISBN: 978-0-2415-3145-7

Printed and bound in China

For the curious
www.dk.com

MIX
Paper from
responsible sources
FSC™ C018179

This book was made with Forest Stewardship Council™ certified paper –
one small step in DK's commitment to a sustainable future.
For more information go to **www.dk.com/our-green-pledge**

Contents

Quick and Easy

**Food for the modern cook – home cooking where convenience is key.
Our modern lives are jam-packed with distractions, whether that be work,
family, the gym, or just finding the time to put on a load of washing. With all
these conflicting obligations, one of the first things sacrificed is your time in
the kitchen and a home-cooked dinner.**

Cooking doesn't need to be hard or time-consuming. Our recipes have been developed with the modern cook in mind, using simple or pre-packaged ingredients and ingenious cooking tricks to get your dinner on the table in no time at all. As we have all become more health-conscious and food-savvy, supermarkets have responded to our concerns with an array of good-quality ready-made products that make all the difference when trying to prepare dinner quickly. Embrace premade sauces, microwaveable grains, and marinated and diced meats, and don't be afraid to purchase something (of good quality) to speed up the cooking process. What is important here is you in the kitchen. Find the joy in being able to make delicious and healthy home-made food, and never rely on takeaway again. All our recipes feature one of the following labels to help guide your meal choices. Also remember to take advantage of the tips and tricks on the opposite page.

CHEAP EAT

A bargain dinner In-season, readily available fresh ingredients are great for budget-conscious cooks.

HEALTHY CHOICE

Better for you This takes all the guesswork out of trying to find fast, healthy food choices.

MEAT-FREE

Veggie meal option Not just for Mondays – meat-free is a great way to start eating more fresh vegetables.

ONE-PAN

Quick clean-up Great for those nights you can't be bothered with multiple pots, pans, and washing up.

GLUTEN-FREE

Coeliac's choice In recipes labelled 'GLUTEN-FREE', all ingredients are safe for those who cannot eat gluten.

DAIRY-FREE

No hidden dairy No dairy products are used – but, if using prepackaged food, read the label carefully.

KID-FRIENDLY

Great for little ones Meals with children in mind, so not too spicy but still full of flavour.

PREP STEPS

1 Quick herbs

To quickly chop soft-leaf herbs (such as flat-leaf parsley, coriander, and dill), use your hands to twist off the stems from the bunch in one go, then chop the leaves and edible stems together.

2 Great grate

To grate vegetables such as carrots and courgettes quickly, use the shredder attachment on a food processor; for cabbage, use the slicer attachment.

3 Acidulated water

This is simply water with lemon juice added. Use it to prevent fennel, apple, and pears from turning brown. Avocado, however, can be stored cut-side down, with the skin on, in plain water to prevent it browning.

4 More juice

For speed and to maximize the amount of juice extracted from lemons and limes, first roll the fruit firmly on a hard bench or work surface using the palm of your hand, or microwave on HIGH (100%) for 15 seconds, before juicing.

5 Herb-ready

Freeze fresh herbs such as thyme, rosemary, and chives, either chopped or in whole-leaf form, in measured quantities in ice-cube trays and covered with a thin layer of olive oil. Simply add the herbs to your recipe straight from the freezer, increasing convenience and cutting down on food wastage.

6 Marinating

To make marinating easier, put the marinating ingredients and the meat or fish in a large zip-top plastic bag; seal the bag and massage the marinade into the ingredients. Leave it in the fridge for at least 3 hours or overnight.

7 Fishy tales

If you aren't a fan of fish skin, there's no need to fuss about trying to remove it before cooking – leave it on, as the skin will hold the delicate flesh of the fish together while it cooks. Peel away the skin when the fish is done; it should lift away easily.

8 Do-ahead

Start the recipe the morning or day before. Measure out the ingredients and store the perishable ones in the fridge. Hard vegetables, with the exception of potatoes, can be cut on the morning of cooking; store covered with damp kitchen paper.

9 Quick clean

For easy cleaning, and to prevent ingredients from sticking, line the bottom of the pan and halfway up the sides with baking parchment. Cook as instructed, then discard the baking parchment when finished.

EXPRESS LUNCHES

Need speedy remedies for what to make for a lunchtime snack or a casual meal with family or friends, or even what to pack for work or the school lunch box? This is the place to go.

Green turkey wraps

GLUTEN-FREE | PREP + COOK TIME **30 MINUTES** | SERVES **4**

Lettuce takes the place of bread in these crunchy wraps. Transport the filled lettuce wraps and green tahini sauce packed separately, to prevent the wraps from becoming soggy, then drizzle with the sauce, roll up to make the wraps, and enjoy.

1 tbsp extra virgin olive oil

1 small orange sweet potato (250g), cut into 1cm rounds

1 small avocado (200g)

1 tbsp lemon juice

200g shaved cooked turkey breast

2 small tomatoes (180g), thinly sliced

1 small carrot (70g), julienned

1 cucumber (130g), julienned

1/2 small red onion (50g), thinly sliced

12 baby cos lettuce leaves (see tip)

green tahini sauce

1/4 cup (70g) tahini

2 tbsp flat-leaf parsley leaves

2 tbsp lemon juice

1 tbsp extra virgin olive oil

1 small garlic clove, crushed

salt and freshly ground black pepper

1 To make the green tahini sauce, stir together the ingredients until smooth; season with salt and pepper to taste. Add a little water, if the mixture is too thick. Set aside.

2 Heat the olive oil in a large non-stick frying pan over a low heat . Cook the sweet potato, turning, for 8 minutes or until tender.

3 Meanwhile, halve the avocado; discard the stone. Thinly slice the avocado flesh, and put in a small bowl with the lemon juice. Toss to coat the avocado in the juice, then drain.

4 Divide the avocado, sweet potato, shaved turkey, tomatoes, carrot, cucumber, and onion evenly among each of the lettuce leaves. Just before serving, drizzle with the green tahini and roll the lettuce around the fillings to enclose.

TIP

You will need 1 or 2 baby cos lettuce, depending on their size.

Prawn cocktail sandwiches with chips

KID-FRIENDLY | PREP + COOK TIME **30 MINUTES** | SERVES **4**

In a classic combination, sweet, juicy prawns and tangy cocktail sauce bring summer to your plate. As usual with a simple dish, it's best to choose good-quality ingredients so that they shine. Also, make sure to choose the most flavourful ripe tomatoes you can find.

800g frozen oven chips

2 tsp olive oil

4 streaky bacon rashers (100g), each cut into three even pieces

1/2 cup (150g) whole-egg mayonnaise

2 tsp tomato ketchup

a few drops of Tabasco

8 slices of white sourdough bread (560g)

1 small green oakleaf lettuce, leaves separated

2 tomatoes (300g), thinly sliced

500g shelled cooked tiger prawns

sea salt flakes

1 Preheat the oven to 220°C (200°C fan/425°F/Gas 7).

2 Arrange the chips in a single layer on a baking tray lined with baking parchment; season with sea salt to taste. Cook in the oven according to the packet directions.

3 Meanwhile, heat the olive oil in a large frying pan over a high heat; cook the bacon for 5 minutes or until crisp. Drain on kitchen paper.

4 Combine the mayonnaise, tomato ketchup, and Tabasco to taste in a small bowl. Spread the bread with the mayonnaise mixture. Sandwich the lettuce, bacon, sliced tomato, and prawns between the bread slices. Serve with the hot chips.

TIP

If you'd like to peel your own prawns, you will need 1kg cooked prawns in the shell. Twist the heads from the prawns, then peel off the shells with the tails; remove the digestive tract.

Chargrilled veggies and butternut dip wraps

GLUTEN-FREE | PREP + COOK TIME **10 MINUTES** | MAKES **4**

These wraps can also be quickly assembled at work for a portable lunch; pack all the ingredients in separate containers, and assemble when you're ready to eat. Not only does this help to avoid soggy wraps, but it keeps the peppery crunch in the rocket as well.

2 x 280g jars chargrilled vegetables in oil

200g tub gluten-free dairy-free Moroccan butternut squash dip or butternut squash hummus (see tip)

4 gluten-free wraps

40g baby rocket leaves

salt and freshly ground black pepper

1   Drain the chargrilled vegetables; pat dry with kitchen paper. Season with salt and pepper to taste.

2   Spread the pumpkin dip onto the wraps; top with the chargrilled vegetables and rocket leaves. Roll up to enclose the fillings.

TIPS

- You can replace the butternut squash dip with red pepper hummus or even baba ghanoush, if you like.
- Use your favourite brand of gluten-free rolls instead of wraps, if you like.
- Make sure to pat the chargrilled vegetables dry with kitchen paper; otherwise the wraps will be soggy by lunchtime if made ahead.

Tuna and olive baguettes

CHEAP EAT | PREP + COOK TIME **10 MINUTES** | MAKES **4**

The complementary pairing of tuna and salty olives used in these baguette sandwiches is one found across the Mediterranean. You could also use a chilli- or lemon-flavoured tuna for the filling. For an even more hunger-satisfying sandwich, add 2 sliced hard-boiled eggs.

2 x 30cm baguettes
1/3 cup (80g) whole-egg mayonnaise
425g can tuna in oil, drained, flaked
1/3 cup (50g) pitted kalamata olives, sliced
1 large tomato (220g), thickly sliced
1/2 small red onion (50g), thinly sliced
1 cucumber (130g), cut into ribbons
2 tbsp micro basil leaves

1 Split open the baguettes without cutting all the way through. Spread the cut sides of the bread with mayonnaise.

2 Sandwich the flaked tuna, olives, tomato, onion, cucumber, and basil leaves between the baguette halves.

3 Cut each baguette in half. Serve cut into smaller pieces, if you like.

TIP

Use your favourite gluten-free bread or wraps, instead of baguettes, if you like.

Veggie and chickpea fritters

MEAT-FREE | PREP + COOK TIME **30 MINUTES** | SERVES **4**

Fritters are a great way to incorporate vegetables into the diet of fussy eaters, and are delicious eaten warm or cold. While we've used mint in the recipe here, any soft-leaf herb such as basil, coriander, or flat-leaf parsley will work well.

400g can chickpeas, drained, rinsed

$^3/_4$ cup (110g) wholemeal self-raising flour

$^1/_2$ cup (125ml) milk

2 eggs

$^3/_4$ cup (120g) frozen peas and sweetcorn mix

1 roasted or chargrilled red pepper in oil, drained, finely chopped

2 spring onions, thinly sliced

1 small courgette (90g), coarsely grated

1 small carrot (70g), coarsely grated

$^1/_2$ cup (60g) coarsely grated Cheddar

2 tbsp coarsely chopped mint leaves

2 tbsp extra virgin olive oil

salt and freshly ground black pepper

1 Blend or process the chickpeas until coarsely chopped.

2 Sift the flour into a medium bowl; add any bran material left in the sieve to the bowl. Lightly whisk together the milk and eggs in a separate, small bowl or jug. Make a well in the centre of the flour; stir in the combined milk-and-egg mixture until smooth. Stir in the chickpeas, peas and sweetcorn mix, red pepper, spring onions, courgette, carrot, Cheddar, and mint. Season with salt and pepper to taste.

3 Heat the olive oil in a large non-stick frying pan over a medium heat. Once the oil is hot, drop $^1/_4$ cup (60ml) batter for each fritter, in batches, into the pan (allow room for the mixture to spread). Cook for 5 minutes or until the fritters are lightly browned on both sides and cooked through.

TIP

Serve the fritters with a spicy tomato chutney and mixed salad leaves, if you like.

Sweet pepper and ricotta frittata

MEAT-FREE | PREP + COOK TIME **30 MINUTES** | SERVES **6**

The frittata can be eaten hot, warm, or at room temperature, making it ideal for a relaxed
lunch, an outdoor picnic, or even a portable lunchtime choice for work. Or do as the Spanish
do and serve any leftover frittata stuffed into rolls with ham and other sandwich trappings.

8 eggs

1/4 cup (60ml) milk

1/3 cup (40g) coarsely grated Cheddar

1 tbsp extra virgin olive oil

1/4 cup (7g) small fresh basil leaves

100g fresh firm ricotta

1 red pepper (200g), thinly sliced

1 green pepper (200g), thinly sliced

salt and freshly ground black pepper

1 Preheat the oven to 220°C (200°C fan/425°F/Gas 7).

2 Whisk together the eggs, milk, and Cheddar in a large jug; season with
salt and pepper to taste.

3 Heat the olive oil in a 17cm (base measurement) ovenproof frying pan
over a medium heat. Add the egg mixture to the pan; cook for 3 minutes,
scraping the edges of the egg into the centre of the pan. Top with the
basil, chunks of the ricotta, and red and green peppers. Cook the
frittata, without stirring, over a medium heat for 2 minutes or until the
bottom and edges are almost set. Transfer the pan to the oven. Bake for
15 minutes or until set and lightly browned. Allow to stand in the pan
for 5 minutes.

4 Slide the frittata onto a serving plate, and cut into wedges to serve.

TIP

You will need a frying pan with an ovenproof handle
for this recipe, or cover the handle with a few layers
of foil to protect it from the heat of the oven.

Creamy chicken and pasta salad

CHEAP EAT | PREP + COOK TIME **30 MINUTES** | SERVES **6**

Whether you're a big kid or a little kid, this refreshing but filling salad would also make a great supper. Double the recipe and not only do you have a simple evening meal at the end of a busy day, but lunch for work the next day is covered as well.

400g skinless boneless chicken breasts

500g large dried pasta shells

2 celery sticks (300g), trimmed, thinly sliced

1 small red onion (100g), thinly sliced

1 cup (120g) roasted pecans

$^1/_2$ cup (90g) thinly sliced dill pickles

50g baby rocket leaves

salt and freshly ground black pepper

creamy tarragon dressing

$^3/_4$ cup (225g) mayonnaise

$^1/_2$ cup (120g) soured cream

2 tbsp lemon juice

1 tbsp finely chopped tarragon

1 Bring 3 cups (750ml) water to the boil in a medium saucepan. Add the whole chicken breasts; simmer, covered, for 10 minutes. Allow the chicken to cool in the poaching liquid for 10 minutes, then drain. Coarsely shred into large, bite-sized pieces.

2 Meanwhile, cook the pasta in a large saucepan of boiling salted water according to the packet directions until almost tender; drain. Rinse under cold running water; drain again.

3 To make the creamy tarragon dressing, combine the ingredients in a small bowl and mix through evenly.

4 Put the pasta in a large bowl with the shredded chicken, tarragon dressing, and the remaining ingredients. Gently toss through. Season with salt and pepper to taste.

TIPS

- Use cornichons or other small gherkins in place of the dill pickles, if you like.
- If you would prefer a vinaigrette dressing, put $^1/_4$ cup (60ml) olive oil, $^1/_4$ cup (60ml) lemon juice, and the finely chopped tarragon in a screw-top jar with a tight-fitting lid; shake well to combine.

Teriyaki chicken rice paper rolls

KID-FRIENDLY/CHEAP EAT | PREP + COOK TIME **30 MINUTES** | MAKES **24**

The trick to assembling Vietnamese-style fresh rice paper rolls is to soak the rice paper wrappers until only just softened. Once they are removed from the water, the wrappers will continue to soften, making them pliable enough to fold easily.

6 chicken thigh fillets (660g)

¼ cup (60ml) teriyaki sauce

4 cucumbers (520g)

200g enoki mushrooms

2 tsp groundnut oil

24 x 17cm square rice paper wrappers

lime and sweet chilli dipping sauce

⅓ cup (80ml) sweet chilli sauce

2 tbsp lime juice

1 Trim the chicken and cut each fillet into 8 strips lengthways. Combine the chicken and marinade in a small bowl. Set aside.

2 Meanwhile, cut the cucumbers in half lengthways; discard the seeds. Cut the cucumber halves in half crossways; cut the pieces into 3 strips lengthways. Trim the enoki mushrooms.

3 Drain the chicken; discard the marinade. Heat the oil in a large frying pan over a medium-high heat; cook the chicken, in batches, for 3 minutes or until cooked through. Allow to cool for 10 minutes.

4 Meanwhile, to make the lime and sweet chilli dipping sauce, combine the ingredients in a small bowl.

5 Once the chicken has cooled, place 1 rice paper wrapper in a medium bowl of warm water until just softened. Lift the wrapper carefully from the water, placing it on a tea-towel-covered board with a corner pointing towards you. Place 2 pieces of the chicken horizontally in the centre of the rice paper wrapper; top with 2 pieces of the cucumber, then a few mushrooms. Fold the corner nearest you over the filling; roll up the rice paper wrapper to enclose the filling, folding in one side after the first complete turn of roll. Repeat with the remaining rice paper wrappers, chicken, cucumber, and mushrooms. Serve the rice paper rolls with the dipping sauce.

TIP

Keep the rice paper rolls fresh by covering them with a slightly damp piece of kitchen paper, then store them in an airtight container in the refrigerator.

Tuna and quinoa niçoise salad

HEALTHY CHOICE | PREP + COOK TIME **30 MINUTES** | SERVES **4**

Quinoa makes an appearance here alongside the more traditional salade niçoise ingredients of tomatoes, eggs, olives, and tuna. This lunch salad can be prepared the night before for an office lunch. Pack the salad and vinaigrette separately, and combine just before serving.

1¹/₂ cups (300g) red quinoa

4 eggs, at room temperature (see tips)

200g green beans, trimmed

425g can tuna in oil, drained, flaked

250g cherry tomatoes, halved

¹/₂ cup (60g) pitted kalamata olives

¹/₂ cup (15g) firmly packed flat-leaf parsley leaves

1 tbsp finely chopped chives

caper and parmesan vinaigrette

1 tbsp drained baby capers, rinsed, chopped

¹/₄ cup (20g) finely grated Parmesan

¹/₄ cup (60ml) white wine vinegar

2 tbsp extra virgin olive oil

1 small garlic clove, crushed

1 tsp Dijon mustard

1 tsp caster sugar

sea salt and freshly ground black pepper

1 Cook the quinoa in a large saucepan of boiling water for 12 minutes or until tender; drain. Set aside to cool.

2 Meanwhile, cook the eggs in a small saucepan of boiling water for 4 minutes until medium-boiled. Drain, then cool the eggs under cold running water. Peel carefully, then halve the eggs. Set aside.

3 Boil, steam, or microwave the green beans until tender; drain. Rinse under cold water to refresh; drain.

4 Meanwhile, to make the caper and Parmesan vinaigrette, combine the ingredients in a small bowl; season with sea salt and pepper to taste.

5 Put the quinoa and beans in a large bowl with the tuna, cherry tomatoes, olives, parsley, and vinaigrette; toss to combine. Serve the quinoa salad topped with the egg halves and the chives sprinkled over the top.

TIP

If you forget to bring the eggs to room temperature first, place them straight from the fridge into a saucepan of cold water; bring to the boil, then boil for 5 minutes. If you want to 'centre' the egg yolks, gently stir the eggs until the water comes to the boil.

Empanada toasties

KID-FRIENDLY | PREP + COOK TIME **30 MINUTES** | MAKES **6**

This speedy adaptation of a beef empanada, echoing the classic South American meat-filled version, uses ready-made filo pastry and a sandwich press for ease. Empanada fillings are many and varied, but this one uses chopped egg and olives in a characteristic flavour boost.

1 egg

1/3 cup (80ml) olive oil

1 small onion (80g), finely chopped

2 garlic cloves, crushed

½ tsp sweet paprika

½ tsp ground coriander

½ tsp ground cumin

½ tsp dried oregano

225g lean beef mince

2 vine-ripened tomatoes, finely chopped

1/3 cup (50g) pimento-stuffed green olives, finely chopped

12 sheets of filo pastry

1 cup (120g) grated Cheddar

salt and freshly ground black pepper

2 tbsp coriander leaves (optional), to serve

adobo mayonnaise

½ cup (150g) whole-egg mayonnaise

1 tbsp chipotle chilli paste

1 Cook the egg in a saucepan of boiling water for 9 minutes or until just hard-boiled; allow to cool. Peel and coarsely chop. Set aside.

2 Heat 1 tablespoon of the oil in a frying pan over a high heat. Add the onion; cook, stirring, for 2 minutes. Add the garlic, paprika, coriander, cumin, and oregano; cook for a further 1 minute until fragrant. Add the beef mince; cook, stirring to break up any lumps, for 3 minutes or until browned and cooked through. Add the tomato; cook, stirring, for 2 minutes or until the liquid is evaporated.

3 Remove the pan from the heat; stir through the chopped egg and olives. Season with salt and pepper to taste; cool slightly to prevent the pastry from becoming soggy when you assemble the empanadas.

4 To make the adobo mayonnaise, stir the ingredients together in a small bowl until combined.

5 On a clean work surface, layer 2 rectangular sheets of the filo pastry, brushing each sheet with a little of the olive oil. Place ¼ cup of the beef mixture and 2 tablespoons of the cheese in a corner of the pastry sheet. Fold the opposite corner of pastry across the filling to form a triangle; fold any excess pastry over and tuck under the triangle. Repeat with the remaining pastry, olive oil, beef mixture, and cheese to make a total of 6 'empanadas'.

6 Preheat a sandwich press. Brush each empanada with a little of the olive oil; cook in the hot sandwich press for 7 minutes until golden and crisp.

7 Cut the empanada toasties in half, and serve with the adobo mayonnaise and coriander leaves sprinkled over the top, if you like.

TIP

Empanada toasties can be cooked to the end of step 6 the night before. You can also freeze them for up to 1 month; thaw in the fridge.

Sweet chilli chicken and BLAT salad

CHEAP EAT | PREP + COOK TIME **25 MINUTES** | SERVES **4**

We've taken the flavours of our favourite lunchtime sandwich and reinvented it as
a substantial salad. If you don't want to forego bread, then simply serve the salad with
sourdough and add lemon wedges for squeezing over to add freshness.

4 skinless boneless chicken breasts (800g)

2 tbsp extra virgin olive oil

¼ cup (125ml) sweet chilli sauce

1 garlic clove, crushed

⅓ cup (80ml) lime juice

8 streaky bacon rashers (200g)

250g cherry vine tomatoes

⅓ cup (100g) mayonnaise

1 tbsp finely chopped flat-leaf parsley

2 baby cos lettuces (360g), leaves separated

1 avocado (250g), thinly sliced lengthways

salt and freshly ground black pepper

1 Preheat an oiled grill plate (or ridged cast-iron grill pan or barbecue) to a medium heat.

2 Combine the chicken, olive oil, sweet chilli sauce, garlic, and half of the lime juice in a medium bowl; season with salt and pepper to taste. Cook the chicken, in batches, on the grill for 5 minutes on each side or until cooked through and grill marks appear. Remove from the heat, cover, and set aside to keep warm.

3 Meanwhile, cook the bacon and tomatoes on the grill over a medium heat until the bacon is crisp and the tomatoes begin to soften.

4 Combine the mayonnaise, remaining lime juice, and parsley in a small bowl; stir to mix through evenly.

5 Arrange the lettuce on 4 serving plates; top with the chicken, bacon, tomatoes, and avocado; drizzle with the dressing. Serve immediately.

TIP

The number-one mistake people make when grilling is being impatient. Allow the chicken enough time before turning it over that it develops char marks and doesn't stick to the grill.

Corn and quinoa chowder

MEAT-FREE | PREP + COOK TIME **30 MINUTES** | SERVES **4**

This contemporary take on corn chowder omits added starch for thickening and instead relies on quinoa to do the job. If you seek out a gluten-free stock and gluten-free tortillas, this recipe is also suitable for coeliac diets.

2 tbsp olive oil

4 corn cobs, trimmed, kernels removed

1 large onion (200g), finely chopped

1 large potato (300g), peeled, coarsely chopped

2 garlic cloves, crushed

1 tsp smoked paprika

1 litre (4 cups) vegetable stock

1/2 cup (125ml) single cream

1/3 cup (70g) red or white quinoa

3/4 cup (180ml) water

1/3 cup (7g) loosely packed coriander leaves

4 x 21cm wholegrain tortillas, toasted, torn

2 limes (130g), halved

salt and freshly ground black pepper

guacamole

1 avocado (250g), coarsely mashed

1 spring onion, thinly sliced

2 tbsp lime juice

1 Heat the oil in a large saucepan over a medium heat; cook the corn, onion, and potato, covered, for 8 minutes until the onion softens. Add the garlic and half of the paprika; cook, stirring, for 1 minute until fragrant.

2 Add the stock and cream; bring to the boil over a high heat. Reduce the heat to medium; cook, covered, for 10 minutes or until the potato is tender. Remove from the heat; allow to stand for 5 minutes. Blend or process half of the chowder until almost smooth; return to the pan. Season with salt and pepper to taste. Stir over the heat until hot.

3 Meanwhile, put the quinoa and 3/4 cup (180ml) water in a small saucepan; bring to the boil. Reduce the heat to low; cook, covered, for 12 minutes until tender. Allow the quinoa to stand, covered, for 10 minutes, then fluff up with a fork. Stir the quinoa through the chowder.

4 Meanwhile, to make the guacamole, combine the avocado, spring onion, and lime juice in a small bowl; season with salt and pepper to taste.

5 Ladle the chowder into 4 serving bowls; top with the guacamole, coriander leaves, and remaining paprika. Serve with the tortillas and lime halves for squeezing over.

TIP

If using a jug blender or food processor to blend the soup, make sure the soup is cool before blending, as the heat of a hot soup can cause the lid to blow off.

Chicken, asparagus, and kale Caesar salad

KID-FRIENDLY | PREP + COOK TIME **30 MINUTES** | SERVES **4**

Classic Caesar salad gets an update with chicken and kale, and green goddess dressing in place of the usual anchovy mayonnaise. The trick to using kale in a salad is to massage the leaves for a few minutes first, either with a little oil and salt, or in the dressing on its own.

12 thin slices of sourdough baguette (100g)

³/₄ cup (80g) finely grated Parmesan

1 tbsp extra virgin olive oil

8 prosciutto slices (120g)

300g fresh asparagus, trimmed, halved lengthways

4 eggs

100g trimmed kale leaves, torn

400g shredded skinless roast or chargrilled chicken

green goddess dressing

¹/₄ cup (75g) whole-egg mayonnaise

2 tbsp soured cream

¹/₄ cup coarsely chopped flat-leaf parsley

1 tbsp coarsely chopped basil

1 tbsp coarsely chopped chives

1 tbsp lemon juice

1 garlic clove, finely chopped

salt and freshly ground black pepper

1 To make the green goddess dressing, process the ingredients until smooth and combined; season with salt and pepper to taste. Set aside.

2 Preheat the grill to a medium heat. Toast the bread on one side, then turn onto the other side and sprinkle with half of the Parmesan. Grill the croutons until the Parmesan melts and is lightly browned. Set aside.

3 Heat the olive oil in a small frying pan over a medium heat; cook the prosciutto until golden and crisp. Remove from the pan; set aside to drain on kitchen paper. Cook the asparagus in the same pan, stirring, for 5 minutes or until lightly browned and tender.

4 Place the eggs in a medium saucepan; cover with cold water. Stir gently (this centres the yolks) over a high heat until the water comes to the boil. Boil for 3 minutes or until soft-boiled. Drain the eggs; rinse under cold water. Roll the eggs on a work surface, then peel.

5 Meanwhile, put the kale and one-quarter of the green goddess dressing in a large bowl; toss to combine. Allow to stand for 5 minutes to soften the kale slightly.

6 Arrange the kale, croutons, chicken, prosciutto, asparagus, remaining Parmesan, and halved soft-boiled eggs on a platter. Drizzle generously with the remaining green goddess dressing.

TIP

For a meat-free meal, omit the chicken and prosciutto; add some more grilled asparagus or chestnut mushrooms instead.

Smoked salmon salad with Japanese dressing

HEALTHY CHOICE | PREP + COOK TIME **25 MINUTES** | SERVES **6**

A zingy dressing and toasted sesame seeds lift this smoked salmon salad out of the ordinary with very little effort. For a portable lunch, the recipe can be prepared up to 8 hours ahead to the end of step 3; cover and refrigerate the salad ingredients until ready to assemble.

340g asparagus, trimmed, cut into short lengths

2 cups (200g) frozen edamame pods, shelled (see tips)

500g small radishes, thinly sliced (see tips)

1 cucumber (400g), thinly sliced (see tips)

200g tatsoi leaves

200g mizuna leaves

50g prepared seaweed salad, optional (see tips)

600g smoked salmon slices

2 tsp sesame seeds, toasted

salt and freshly ground black pepper

Japanese dressing

1 tbsp grated fresh ginger

1/4 cup (60ml) extra virgin olive oil

1/4 cup (60ml) mirin

1/4 cup (60ml) soy sauce

2 tbsp lime juice

1 tbsp finely grated palm sugar

1 small red chilli, seeded, finely chopped

1 Cook the asparagus and edamame in a medium saucepan of boiling water for 30 seconds or until just tender. Remove with a slotted spoon. Refresh in a bowl of iced water; drain and set aside.

2 To make the Japanese dressing, press the ginger between 2 spoons over a small bowl or jug to extract the juice; discard the pulp. Transfer the ginger juice to a small screw-top jar with a tight-fitting lid. Add the remaining dressing ingredients; shake well to combine.

3 Put the radish, cucumber, tatsoi and mizuna leaves, asparagus, edamame, and seaweed salad, if using, in a large bowl.

4 Transfer the salad to a platter or divide evenly among 6 plates; top with the salmon. Drizzle the salad with the Japanese dressing, and sprinkle with the toasted sesame seeds. Season with salt and pepper to taste.

TIPS

- You will need 1/2 cup (100g) shelled edamame. Use a V-slicer or mandolin to thinly slice the radishes and cucumber, if you have one.
- Seaweed salad is available from fishmongers, sushi bars, and salad bars.
- You can use smoked sea trout instead of the salmon and watercress, or spinach leaves instead of the tatsoi and mizuna, if you like.

Chickpea tabbouleh with beetroot

MEAT-FREE | PREP + COOK TIME **20 MINUTES** | SERVES **6**

A Middle Eastern salad especially popular in Lebanon, tabbouleh is usually made with bulgur wheat. Cooked chickpeas are used here instead, cutting down preparation time by avoiding the need for soaking. A simple yogurt dressing adds the characteristic lemony acidity.

2 x 400g cans chickpeas, drained, rinsed

250g cherry vine tomatoes, halved

1 large beetroot (200g), peeled, julienned

1 small red onion (100g), halved, thinly sliced

2 tbsp extra virgin olive oil

1/2 cup (50g) walnuts, roasted, chopped

1/2 cup (15g) firmly packed flat-leaf parsley leaves

1/2 cup (15g) firmly packed small mint leaves

1 tsp grated lemon zest (see tip)

salt and freshly ground black pepper

lemon-yogurt dressing

1/2 cup (140g) Greek-style yogurt

1/2 tsp finely grated lemon zest

1 tbsp lemon juice

1 Process the chickpeas using the pulse button until finely chopped to about the size of barley.

2 Meanwhile, to make the lemon-yogurt dressing, combine the ingredients in a small bowl; season with salt and pepper to taste. Set aside.

3 Put the chickpeas, tomatoes, beetroot, onion, olive oil, walnuts, parsley, and mint in a large bowl; toss gently to combine. Season with salt and pepper to taste. Drizzle with the lemon-yogurt dressing, and sprinkle over the lemon zest.

TIPS

- Use a julienne peeler to shred the beetroot into fine julienne more easily.
- You could use a zesting tool to create strips of lemon zest instead of grating. If you don't have one, use a vegetable peeler to remove the zest, avoiding the white pith, then cut the zest into long, thin strips.

Green mango slaw with chilli-lime dressing

HEALTHY CHOICE | PREP + COOK TIME **25 MINUTES + STANDING** | SERVES **8 AS A SIDE**

This fragrant Thai-inspired slaw is at once sour, sweet, and salty, and delightfully crisp.
Ideally, add the dressing at the last minute before serving, to keep the salad at its crispest.
It can be eaten as it is or stuffed into baps with sliced ham or pork as a delicious sandwich.

1/4 red cabbage (330g), thinly sliced

1 large carrot (180g), peeled, julienned

1 large green or firm, underripe mango, peeled, julienned (see tip)

5 shallots, thinly sliced

1 cup (150g) frozen shelled edamame, thawed

1/3 cup (10g) firmly packed mint leaves

1/3 cup (10g) Thai basil leaves

1/4 cup (40g) sesame seeds, toasted

chilli-lime dressing

1/3 cup (80ml) lime juice

2 tbsp grapeseed oil

1 tbsp fish sauce

30g palm sugar, finely grated

2 long red chillies, seeded, finely chopped

salt and freshly ground black pepper

1   Spread the cabbage, in a single layer, over a baking tray. Allow to stand at room temperature for 30 minutes to dry (this will help to stop the colour bleeding into the rest of the salad).

2   Put the cabbage, carrot, green mango, shallots, edamame, herbs, and sesame seeds in a large bowl.

3   To make the chilli-lime dressing, put the ingredients in a screw-top jar with a tight-fitting lid. Shake well until the sugar dissolves. Season with salt and pepper to taste.

4   Just before serving, drizzle the chilli-lime dressing over the salad; toss gently to combine.

TIPS

• If you want a creamy slaw, add a little Japanese mayonnaise to the dressing.
• To make this salad vegetarian, swap the fish sauce for soy sauce.
• You can use either green papaya or jicama instead of the mango, if you like.

Asparagus with crisp lentils and herby yogurt

MEAT-FREE | PREP + COOK TIME **30 MINUTES** | SERVES **6**

The lentils in this recipe are cooked until crisp, taking on a different life both as a protein
and as a crunchy topping to add layers of contrasting texture with the tender fresh asparagus
and creamy dressing. This technique can also be used with canned butterbeans.

2 x 400g cans brown lentils, drained, rinsed

1/3 cup (80ml) extra virgin olive oil

1 garlic clove, crushed

1 long red chilli, seeded, finely chopped

1 lemon (140g)

680g asparagus, trimmed

salt and freshly ground black pepper

herb yogurt

1 cup (280g) Greek-style yogurt

1 cup (25g) firmly packed flat-leaf
parsley leaves

1/4 cup (6g) tarragon

2 tbsp lemon juice

1 Pat the lentils dry with kitchen paper. Heat the oil in a large frying pan
over a medium-high heat. Cook the garlic and chilli for 30 seconds until
fragrant. Add the lentils; cook, stirring, for 15 minutes or until the lentils
are crisp. Season with salt and pepper to taste. Remove the lentils from
the pan, and set aside to drain on kitchen paper.

2 Remove strips of zest from the lemon using a zesting tool; place in a bowl
of cold water.

3 Put half of the asparagus in a steamer, bamboo steamer, or round wire
rack over a wok or wide pan containing about 2cm water. Steam the
asparagus, covered, for 1 minute; transfer to a plate. Season with salt
and pepper to taste. Repeat with the remaining asparagus.

4 Meanwhile, to make the herb yogurt, pulse half of the yogurt, parsley,
tarragon, and lemon juice in a small food processor until smooth.
Transfer to a small bowl; stir in the remaining yogurt; season with salt
and pepper to taste.

5 Spoon some of the herb yogurt onto a platter. Top with the asparagus,
then sprinkle with the crisp lentils. Spoon over more of the herb yogurt;
top with the lemon zest strips. Serve with the remaining herb yogurt for
spooning over.

TIP

The herb yogurt can be made up to a day
ahead and refrigerated until needed.

Fast salads

Fresh, fast, and balanced in flavour and wholefood nutrition, these salads make great go-to options when you need to get food to the table fast or are looking for inspiration for a portable lunch. Colourful and appealing, they also work well as part of a larger meal.

Moroccan vegetable salad

PREP TIME **20 MINUTES** | SERVES **4**

Using the shredder attachment on a food processor, grate 2 uncooked, peeled beetroot, 1 bunch of radishes, 2 courgettes, and 1 large carrot; tip the vegetables onto a platter. Wipe the food processor bowl clean. Process $1/3$ cup (80ml) extra virgin olive oil, 2 tablespoons pomegranate molasses, 2 tablespoons lemon juice, $1/2$ teaspoon each of ground cumin, sumac, and salt to taste until combined. Drizzle half of the dressing over the vegetables. Rinse and drain a 400g can chickpeas; combine with the remaining dressing and 250g halved cherry tomatoes in a medium bowl. Top the salad with the chickpea mixture; sprinkle with $1/2$ cup (10g) loosely packed mint leaves. Serve with $1 1/2$ cups (100g) pitta chips.

Salad of crunchy things

PREP + COOK TIME **20 MINUTES** | SERVES **4**

In a small frying pan over a medium heat, stir 1 tablespoon olive oil and 2 tablespoons each of sesame seeds, sunflower seeds, and pepitas for 5 minutes until golden. Add 2 teaspoons chia seeds and 1 tablespoon tamari; stir to combine. Remove from the heat. Using the shredder attachment on a food processor, grate 2 peeled kohlrabi and 400g trimmed Brussels sprouts. Tip the vegetables into a large bowl. Process 4 purple kale leaves until coarsely chopped; add to the bowl with $3/4$ cup (15g) loosely packed flat-leaf parsley leaves. Process $1/4$ cup (60ml) extra virgin olive oil, 2 tablespoons lemon juice, 1 crushed garlic clove, and 2 teaspoons Dijon mustard; season with salt and pepper to taste. Add to the vegetables, and toss through. Top with the crunchy seed mixture.

Vietnamese chicken salad

PREP TIME **30 MINUTES** | SERVES **4**

Using the shredder attachment on a food processor, grate 200g white cabbage; transfer to a small bowl. Grate 1 large carrot; tip into a large bowl. Add 1 thinly sliced red onion, $1/2$ cup (125ml) rice wine vinegar, 2 teaspoons salt, and 2 tablespoons caster sugar; allow to stand for 5 minutes. Add $1 1/2$ cups (175g) beansprouts; allow to stand for 3 minutes. Drain the pickled vegetables; return to the bowl. Add the cabbage, 500g shredded cooked skinless chicken breast, and $1/3$ cup (10g) each of mint and coriander leaves. Put $1/4$ cup (60ml) water, 1 crushed garlic clove, 2 tablespoons each of fish sauce, caster sugar, and lime juice in a screw-top jar; shake well. Pour over the salad; toss to combine. Sprinkle with 2 tablespoons each of crushed salted roasted cashews and fried shallots.

Red salad

PREP TIME **30 MINUTES** | SERVES **4**

Using the slicer attachment on a food processor, slice 1 red onion and $1/2$ red cabbage. Whisk together $2/3$ cup (80ml) white wine vinegar and $1/4$ cup (55g) caster sugar in a large bowl until the sugar dissolves. Add the cabbage mixture; allow to stand for 20 minutes. Drain and discard any excess dressing from the bowl; season the vegetable mixture with salt and freshly ground black pepper to taste. Cut 250g precooked beetroot into wedges. Cut 2 small radicchio into thin wedges; arrange on a platter with the beetroot and cabbage mixture. Crumble over 150g soft goat's cheese; top with $1/4$ cup (40g) coarsely chopped dry-roasted almonds and $1/4$ cup (15g) chopped chives. Drizzle with 1 tablespoon extra virgin olive oil.

Smoked trout and pickled vegetable buns

HEALTHIER CHOICE | PREP + COOK TIME **20 MINUTES + REFRIGERATION** | SERVES **6**

Quick-pickled vegetables add crunch and a sharp tang to these rolls. To make the recipe an even healthier choice, choose a wholegrain roll and, depending on your dietary preferences, substitute the fish for smoked chicken or even marinated tofu, if you like.

6 sourdough bread rolls, halved

1 cup (240g) spreadable cream cheese

1 baby cos lettuce (180g), leaves separated

480g hot-smoked trout or salmon fillets, flaked

pickled veg

$1/3$ cup (80ml) lemon juice

2 tbsp caster sugar

2 tbsp finely chopped fresh dill

1 tbsp mustard seeds, toasted

1 tbsp white wine vinegar

2 tsp sea salt flakes

8 small radishes (280g), thinly sliced

1 small red onion (100g), thinly sliced into rings

4 baby cucumbers (160g), thinly sliced lengthways

freshly ground black pepper

1 To make the pickled veg, put the lemon juice, caster sugar, dill, mustard seeds, vinegar, and sea salt in a medium glass or non-reactive bowl. Whisk together until the sugar dissolves. Add the radishes, onion, and cucumbers. Season with pepper to taste; toss to combine. Cover the pickles; refrigerate for 30 minutes to allow the flavours to develop. Drain, discarding the pickling liquid.

2 Spread the bread roll bases with the cream cheese; layer with the lettuce, trout, and pickled vegetables. Top with the bread roll lids.

3 Arrange the buns on a large platter, and serve immediately.

TIPS

• Use a mandolin or V-slicer, available from kitchenware stores, to thinly slice the vegetables.

• For decoration and ease of handling, either tie the rolls with kitchen string or secure them with skewers, if you like.

Roasted chickpea and carrot salad with feta

MEAT-FREE | PREP + COOK TIME **30 MINUTES** | SERVES **1**

To speed preparation, get the carrots into the oven first. While they are cooking, pick the herbs so they're ready to use. You could make a double quantity, and take the other half to lunch the following day – or bulk up the quantities even more to serve family or friends.

1 bunch of baby carrots (185g), trimmed

400g can chickpeas, drained, rinsed

2 tbsp extra virgin olive oil

1 tsp finely grated lemon zest

1½ tsp cumin seeds, lightly crushed

1½ tsp coriander seeds, lightly crushed

1½ tsp fennel seeds, lightly crushed

½ cup (10g) loosely packed mint leaves

½ cup (10g) loosely packed flat-leaf parsley

¼ cup (6g) loosely packed dill sprigs

2 tbsp lemon juice

100g drained marinated feta,
plus 1 tbsp of the marinating oil

salt and freshly ground black pepper

crusty bread, to serve

1 Preheat the oven to 220°C (200°C fan/425°F/Gas 7).

2 Combine the carrots, chickpeas, oil, lemon zest, and seeds on a baking tray lined with baking parchment; season with salt and pepper to taste. Roast in the oven for 25 minutes or until the carrots are golden and tender. Transfer the carrots to a serving bowl.

3 Combine the mint, parsley, and dill in a small bowl. Drizzle with the lemon juice; season with salt and pepper to taste. Sprinkle the herbs over the carrot and chickpea mixture. Top with the feta, then drizzle with a little of the marinating oil. Accompany with crusty bread, if you like.

TIP

If you buy a bunch of carrots with the green tops attached, trim them off before you put the carrots in the vegetable crisper of the refrigerator. This helps to extend their shelf life.

Cheesy chorizo quesaditas

KID-FRIENDLY | PREP + COOK TIME **20 MINUTES** | MAKES **2**

Oozy with cheese and spicy, paprika-laden chorizo, these mini quesadillas are simple to put together. Baby spinach, onion, and red pepper provide balance in both flavour and texture. The end result: a hearty lunch in its own edible container.

1 tbsp olive oil

1 small red onion, finely chopped

200g cured chorizo, finely chopped

1 tsp smoked paprika

1/3 cup (80g) chopped drained roasted red pepper in oil

2 wholemeal pitta pockets

1/2 cup (50g) grated mozzarella

1/2 cup (50g) grated Cheddar

1/2 cup (20g) baby spinach leaves

salt and freshly ground black pepper

1 Heat the olive oil in a medium frying pan over a medium-high heat; cook the onion, stirring, for 3 minutes or until softened. Add the chorizo; cook for 2 minutes or until golden. Add the paprika; cook for 30 seconds. Stir in the red pepper; season with salt and pepper to taste.

2 Warm the pitta pockets in a microwave to refresh. Split open the pitta pockets. Fill each with a quarter of the cheese, half of the chorizo mixture, and half of the spinach, then top with the remaining cheese.

3 Preheat a sandwich press until hot. Toast the quesaditas in the sandwich press for 4 minutes or until golden and crisp. Serve immediately.

TIP

For a portable lunch, wrap the quesaditas in baking parchment and pack in airtight containers. Alternatively, pack the ingredients in separate airtight containers to assemble at work. Transport in cooler bags. Refrigerate until ready to toast, then continue with step 3.

Spicy miso dumpling soup

ONE-POT | PREP + COOK TIME **15 MINUTES** | SERVES **2**

Shiro miso is subtler and more delicate than darker miso varieties. Along with chilli and ginger, it provides the defining flavour in this delicious, fast-to-whip-up soup. If you would like to up the vegetable quota, try adding broccoli florets or snow peas (mangetout).

2 tbsp shiro miso (white miso) paste

1 long red chilli, thinly sliced

1 tsp finely grated fresh root ginger

2 tsp light soy sauce

10 frozen pork gyoza

2 baby pak choi (150g), quartered

1 spring onion, thinly sliced diagonally

1 tsp sesame seeds, toasted

1 Put 3 cups (750ml) water and the shiro miso, chilli, ginger, and soy sauce in a small saucepan over a medium heat. Bring to a simmer, stirring occasionally, until well combined.

2 Add the gyoza; cook for 6 minutes or until heated through. Add the pak choi; cook for a further 2 minutes. Spoon into 2 serving bowls. Serve topped with the spring onion and toasted sesame seeds.

TIPS

• You can use vegetarian or chicken gyoza instead of the pork, if you like.

• Miso paste will keep stored in the fridge for up to 3 months and can be used in marinades, stir-fries, and dressings.

WEEKNIGHT FEASTS

These tempting dishes are high in culinary comfort, but low on fuss – just what's needed at the end of a hectic day, whether you're cooking for one or feeding a hungry horde.

Dukkah prawn skewers with labneh and minty tomato salad

HEALTHY CHOICE/GLUTEN-FREE | PREP + COOK TIME **30 MINUTES** | SERVES **4**

Dukkah is an Egyptian spice mixture made of roasted nuts, seeds, and an array of spices. Used as a condiment, dip, or seasoning, variations abound – sometimes even from family to family. In this recipe we've used one that features pistachios, but any dukkah will work.

1.2kg large uncooked king prawns

1/4 cup (35g) pistachio dukkah

2 tbsp extra virgin olive oil

2 garlic cloves, crushed

2 tsp finely grated lemon zest

280g labneh

1 lemon (140g), cut into wedges

minty tomato salad

400g mixed baby heirloom tomatoes, coarsely chopped

1 cup (25g) flat-leaf parsley leaves

1/2 cup (15g) firmly packed mint leaves

2 tbsp red wine vinegar

1 tbsp garlic oil

salt and freshly ground black pepper

1 Shell and devein the prawns, leaving the tails intact.

2 Combine the dukkah, oil, garlic, and lemon zest in a large bowl. Add the prawns; toss to coat in the dukkah mixture.

3 Preheat an oiled grill plate (or ridged cast-iron grill pan or barbecue) to a high heat. Thread the prawns onto 8 bamboo skewers. Cook the skewers on a heated oiled grill plate for 3–4 minutes until the prawns change colour and are just cooked.

4 Meanwhile, to make the minty tomato salad, put the ingredients in a large bowl; toss gently to combine. Season with salt and pepper to taste.

5 Serve the prawn skewers with the salad, labneh, and lemon wedges for squeezing over.

TIPS

- To save time, buy cleaned and shelled prawns from your fishmonger; you will need 600g.
- If you have a nut allergy, substitute the dukkah with 2 teaspons sumac or chopped flat-leaf parsley.
- Cover the ends of the bamboo skewers in foil, to prevent scorching during cooking. Or, if you have time, soak skewers in boiling water for 10 minutes.

Bacon and corn fritters with avocado dressing

KID-FRIENDLY | PREP + COOK TIME **30 MINUTES** | SERVES **4**

We have paired these fritters with fennel, which has an anise-like taste and crisp texture when raw, making it a great companion to cut through richer flavours such as the bacon and creamy avocado dressing used in this recipe.

125g rindless thick bacon rashers, coarsely chopped

125g can corn kernels, drained, rinsed

400g ripe tomatoes, finely chopped

2 garlic cloves, crushed

2 tbsp chopped chives, plus extra 1 tbsp

2 tsp smoked paprika

2 eggs

1/3 cup (80ml) milk

1 cup (150g) spelt flour

1/2 tsp baking powder

2 tbsp olive oil

1 large fennel bulb (550g), thinly sliced

salt and freshly ground black pepper

lemon halves, to serve (optional)

avocado dressing

1 avocado (250g)

1/2 cup (150g) whole-egg mayonnaise

1 tbsp lemon juice

1 garlic clove, crushed

1 Heat a large, non-stick frying pan over a high heat; cook the bacon until golden and crisp. Transfer to a large bowl.

2 Add the corn, tomatoes, garlic, the 2 tablespoons chopped chives, smoked paprika, eggs, and milk; stir to combine. Sift together the spelt flour and baking powder; add to the bowl. Season with salt and pepper to taste, and stir to combine. Set aside.

3 Meanwhile, to make the avocado dressing, blend or process the avocado flesh, mayonnaise, lemon juice, and garlic until smooth. Season with salt and pepper to taste.

4 Heat the olive oil in the same frying pan as the bacon over a medium heat. Spoon 2 tablespoons of the fritter mixture into the pan; cook for 2 minutes or until bubbles appear on top. Turn the fritters; cook for a further 2 minutes until the other side is lightly browned. Repeat with the remaining batter to make 8 fritters in total.

5 Combine the fennel and extra 1 tablespoon chopped chives in a small bowl. Season with salt and pepper to taste.

6 Serve the fritters with the fennel salad, avocado mixture, and lemon halves for squeezing over, if you like.

TIP

If preparing the fennel ahead, drop it into a bowl of iced water and refrigerate until needed, to avoid browning. Drain and pat dry just before using.

Spinach and ricotta-stuffed chicken

ONE-PAN/KID-FRIENDLY | PREP + COOK TIME **30 MINUTES** | SERVES **4**

The topping used for this dish is a classic combination in Italian cooking. The tangy acidity of the tomato cuts through the rich creaminess of the cheese, melding the two together to provide the perfect complement to the chicken.

750g frozen sweet potato chips

1$^1/_3$ cups (320g) fresh ricotta

$^1/_4$ cup (20g) finely grated Parmesan

150g baby spinach leaves

8 x 125g chicken escalopes (see tips)

$^1/_4$ cup (60ml) olive oil

1 cup (260g) bottled passata

1 cup (100g) coarsely grated mozzarella

2 tbsp balsamic dressing

sea salt flakes

1   Preheat the oven to 220°C (200°C fan/425°F/Gas 7).

2   Place the chips on a baking tray lined with baking parchment; season with sea salt flakes. Cook in the oven according to the packet directions until golden and crisp.

3   Meanwhile, mix together the ricotta and Parmesan. Divide 40g of the spinach and the ricotta mixture evenly among the chicken escalopes, leaving a 1cm border around the edges. Roll up to enclose the filling; secure with toothpicks or cocktail sticks.

4   Heat the olive oil in a large frying pan over a medium heat. Cook the chicken, in batches, for 2 minutes on each side or until golden. Remove with a slotted spoon; drain on kitchen paper.

5   Arrange the chicken in a single layer in an oiled shallow large baking dish; top with the passata and mozzarella. Bake for 10 minutes or until the cheese melts and the chicken is cooked through.

6   Toss the remaining spinach with the balsamic dressing in a large bowl.

7   Serve the chicken with the sweet potato chips and spinach salad.

TIPS

• Remove the toothpicks from the chicken before serving.

• If escalopes are unavailable, cut 4 large skinless boneless chicken breasts in half horizontally, to make 8 escalopes, then pound between cling film until even and 5mm thick.

Rosemary turkey skewers

HEALTHY CHOICE | PREP + COOK TIME **30 MINUTES** | SERVES **4**

We've used minced turkey meat for the skewers here, proof that this wonderfully healthy meat shouldn't be reserved just for Christmas day! The rosemary skewers will infuse the meat during cooking; alternatively you can use bamboo skewers and add 2 teaspoons finely chopped rosemary to the mince mixture, if you like.

8 sprigs of rosemary

600g minced turkey

1 egg

2 garlic cloves, crushed

1 tbsp tomato purée

1 cup (70g) stale breadcrumbs

2 tbsp extra virgin olive oil

1 large onion (200g), thinly sliced

1 tbsp plain flour

1 cup (250ml) beef stock

2 tomatoes (300g), coarsely chopped

450g packet white or brown microwave or instant rice

200g green beans, trimmed

1 Remove two-thirds of the leaves from the bottom part of each rosemary sprig to make skewers. Finely chop 2 teaspoons of the leaves; reserve.

2 Combine the turkey, egg, garlic, tomato purée, breadcrumbs, and reserved chopped rosemary in a medium bowl. Mould the turkey mixture into sausage shapes around the rosemary skewers.

3 Preheat an oiled ridged cast-iron grill pan or plate (or a grill or barbecue) to a medium-high heat. Cook the skewers, turning, for 10 minutes or until browned and cooked through. Remove from the pan; cover and set aside to keep warm.

4 Meanwhile, heat the olive oil in a large frying pan over a medium heat; cook the onion, stirring, until soft. Add the flour; cook, stirring, until the mixture bubbles and thickens. Gradually stir in the stock until smooth. Add the tomatoes; cook, stirring, until the gravy boils and thickens.

5 At the same time, heat the rice according to the packet directions. Microwave the green beans on HIGH (100%) for 1 minute or until tender.

6 Serve the skewers with the gravy, rice, and green beans.

Soy-glazed salmon with greens

HEALTHY CHOICE | PREP + COOK TIME **25 MINUTES** | SERVES **1**

Cooking fish with the skin on can be helpful in keeping the fish moist during cooking and
therefore protecting it from being overdone. The skin can always be removed afterwards,
if you prefer, as we've done in the recipe here.

1/4 cup (60ml) soy sauce

2 tbsp caster sugar

2 tsp finely grated fresh root ginger

1 tsp sesame oil

2 tbsp rice wine vinegar

200g boneless salmon fillet, skin on

2 stems of choi sum (55g), coarsely chopped

1/2 cup (50g) sugarsnap peas

1/4 cup (40g) frozen garden peas, thawed

2 tbsp coriander, coarsely chopped,
plus extra leaves, to serve

2 spring onions, thinly sliced diagonally

1 tsp sesame seeds, toasted

steamed brown rice, to serve (optional)

1 Preheat the oven to 220°C (200°C fan/425°F/Gas 7).

2 Combine the soy sauce, sugar, ginger, sesame oil, and half of the vinegar
in a small saucepan; cook the marinade, over a high heat, for 4 minutes
or until thickened.

3 Place the salmon on a small baking tray lined with baking parchment;
brush half of the marinade over the salmon. Roast in the oven for
8 minutes or until golden and almost cooked through.

4 Meanwhile, bring a large saucepan of salted water to the boil. Add the
choi sum; cook for 1 minute. Add the sugarsnap peas and garden peas;
cook for a further minute or until the vegetables are tender crisp. Drain
well; transfer to a serving bowl with the coriander and spring onions.

5 Flake the salmon, discarding the skin. Add to a bowl with the remaining
marinade and vinegar; toss gently to combine.

6 Top with the sesame seeds and extra coriander, and serve with steamed
brown rice, if you like.

Lamb chops with peach caprese salad

GLUTEN-FREE | PREP + COOK TIME **25 MINUTES** | SERVES **4**

This main-course spin-off of the Italian classic caprese salad includes succulent peaches and a vibrant minty pesto. With its fresh mix of flavours and textures that bring summer to your plate, it is ideal for informal eating or a long, lazy lunch, yet so easy to prepare.

8 lamb loin chops (800g)

1$^{1}/_{2}$ tbsp extra virgin olive oil

4 peaches (600g), thickly sliced

250g buffalo mozzarella, torn

400g baby heirloom tomatoes, halved

$^{1}/_{2}$ cup (10g) small basil leaves

1 tbsp white wine vinegar

salt and freshly ground black pepper

pistachio-mint pesto

1$^{1}/_{2}$ cups (35g) firmly packed mint leaves

1 cup (25g) firmly packed flat-leaf parsley leaves

$^{1}/_{2}$ cup (75g) pistachios

1 garlic clove, crushed

2 tsp finely grated lemon zest

2 tsp lemon juice

$^{1}/_{2}$ cup (125ml) extra virgin olive oil

1 To make the pistachio-mint pesto, blend or process the ingredients until smooth; season with salt and pepper to taste.

2 Combine the lamb and 1 tablespoon of the olive oil in a medium bowl; season with salt and pepper to taste. Preheat a lightly oiled ridged cast-iron grill pan or plate (or a grill or barbecue) to a medium-high heat. Cook the lamb for about 3 minutes on each side, adding the peaches to the grill for the last 2 minutes of the lamb cooking time, or until the lamb is cooked as desired and the peaches are golden and grill marks appear.

3 Layer the peaches with the mozzarella, tomatoes, and basil; drizzle with the combined vinegar and remaining oil. Serve the salad with the lamb and pistachio-mint pesto.

TIPS

- Buffalo mozzarella has a tangier flavour than cow's milk mozzarella, which may be substituted for it.
- You could use figs, apples, or pears instead of peaches, if peaches are unavailable.
- For a nut-free pesto, use pepitas (pumpkin seeds) instead of the pistachios.

Lemongrass and lime prawns with broccoli rice

GLUTEN-FREE | PREP + COOK TIME **15 MINUTES** | SERVES **4**

This low-carb recipe replaces white rice with a plant-based rice made from broccoli to accompany the zesty prawns. You could also make this using cauliflower rice. The earthy, slightly bitter flavour of both these vegetables complements the sweetness of the prawns.

500g broccoli, finely chopped

80g butter, chopped

10cm piece of fresh lemongrass (20g), finely chopped

500g shelled medium uncooked prawns

1 tbsp finely grated lime zest

2 tbsp lime juice

2 tbsp finely chopped coriander

2 spring onions, thinly sliced

salt and freshly ground black pepper

2 limes, halved, to serve

1 Process the broccoli, in batches, until finely chopped and resembling rice grains. Blanch in a medium saucepan of boiling water for 20 seconds; drain. Spread out the broccoli on kitchen paper to dry; season with salt and pepper to taste. Cover to keep warm.

2 Melt the butter in a large frying pan over a medium heat; cook the lemongrass, stirring, for 1 minute until fragrant. Increase the heat to high; add the prawns and half of the lime zest. Cook, stirring, for 2–3 minutes until the prawns change colour. Remove from the heat; stir in the lime juice and coriander.

3 Top the broccoli rice with the prawn mixture, remaining lime zest, and spring onions. Serve with the lime halves for squeezing over.

Thai chicken omelettes

HEALTHY CHOICE | PREP + COOK TIME **30 MINUTES** | SERVES **4**

These lacy omelettes are made by drizzling the egg mixture into a wok. You could also put the egg mixture in a squeeze bottle if you have one, and use a small frying pan in place of a wok. Delicate enoki mushrooms impart a milder flavour here than other, earthier mushrooms.

2 tbsp groundnut oil

400g skinless boneless chicken breasts, thinly sliced

1 small onion (80g), thinly sliced

2 garlic cloves, crushed

2 tbsp oyster sauce

8 eggs

1 tsp fish sauce

1 tsp all-purpose soy sauce

100g enoki mushrooms, trimmed (see tips)

1/2 cup (10g) mint leaves

1/2 cup (15g) Thai basil leaves

1 cup (80g) beansprouts

2 limes, cut into wedges

1   Heat 2 teaspoons of the groundnut oil in a wok over a high heat; stir-fry the chicken, in batches, for 3 minutes or until browned. Remove from the wok and set aside.

2   Heat another 2 teaspoons of the groundnut oil in the wok; stir-fry the onion and garlic for 1 minute until fragrant. Return the chicken to the wok with the oyster sauce; stir-fry until hot. Remove from the wok; cover to keep warm while making the omelettes.

3   Whisk together the eggs, fish sauce, and soy sauce in a large jug. Heat 1 teaspoon of the groundnut oil in the same wok, still over a high heat. Put the egg mixture in a plastic zip-top bag. Snip a small hole in one corner and drizzle 1/4 cup (60ml) of the egg mixture into the heated wok; cook until almost set (this happens nearly instantly). Transfer the omelette to a serving plate; cover to keep warm. Repeat the cooking to make a total of 8 omelettes.

4   Fill the omelettes with the chicken mixture, enoki mushrooms, mint, Thai basil, and beansprouts. Serve with the lime wedges for squeezing over.

TIPS

- Enoki mushrooms have clumps of long, spaghetti-like stems with tiny, snowy white caps. They are available from Asian food stores and supermarkets. To trim them, cut off the base clump, leaving the stems long.
- You can use coriander if Thai basil is unavailable.
- If you like it spicy, add some sliced red chilli to your chicken omelettes before serving.

Bacon and herb lamb patties

KID-FRIENDLY | PREP + COOK TIME **25 MINUTES** | MAKES **8**

Taking this recipe one step further to make a pattie roll couldn't be simpler. Spread a fresh bread roll (or a pitta pocket or wrap) with extra tomato chutney or even hummus, and add a sliced pattie, either warm or cold, with some salad.

1 garlic clove, crushed

2 spring onions, finely chopped

500g lean lamb mince

1 egg

¾ cup (50g) wholemeal breadcrumbs

2 tbsp finely chopped flat-leaf parsley

2 tbsp finely chopped oregano

⅓ cup (110g) tomato chutney

8 streaky bacon rashers (200g)

2 tbsp olive oil

salt and freshly ground black pepper

60g watercress, sprigs picked, to serve

1 Combine the garlic, onion, lamb, egg, breadcrumbs, herbs, and chutney in a large bowl; season with salt and pepper to taste. Shape the mixture into 8 patties. Wrap each patty in a bacon rasher. Secure with toothpicks or cocktail sticks.

2 Heat the olive oil in a large frying pan over a medium heat. Cook the patties for 3 minutes on each side or until browned and cooked through. Remove and discard the toothpicks. Serve the warm patties with the watercress alongside.

TIP

Freeze individual cooked and cooled patties in airtight containers for up to 1 month. Thaw overnight in the fridge; reheat in the microwave at work, or eat at room temperature, if taking to school.

Mongolian beef with noodles

ONE-PAN | PREP + COOK TIME **25 MINUTES** | SERVES **4**

Achieving a great stir-fry involves two key steps. First, ensure you have everything ready before you start cooking, so that once the first ingredient hits the wok the process is seamless. Secondly, don't crowd the wok with the meat or it will stew rather than brown.

600g beef fillet, thinly sliced

1/3 cup (80ml) sweet sherry

2 tbsp dark soy sauce

2 tbsp sweet chilli sauce

2 tbsp vegetable oil

1 large onion (200g), thinly sliced

2 garlic cloves, crushed

1 red pepper (200g), thinly sliced

235g choi sum, cut into 10cm lengths

1 tbsp light soft brown sugar

1 tsp sesame oil

1/3 cup (80ml) chicken stock

400g thick hokkien noodles

1   Combine the beef with half each of the sherry, soy sauce, and sweet chilli sauce in a medium bowl.

2   Heat half of the vegetable oil in a wok over a high heat; stir-fry the beef, in batches, for 2 minutes or until browned. Remove from the wok.

3   Heat the remaining vegetable oil in the wok; stir-fry the onion and garlic for 3 minutes or until the onion softens. Add the red pepper and choi sum; stir-fry until the vegetables are tender.

4   Return the beef to the wok with the remaining ingredients; stir-fry for 2 minutes until heated through. Serve immediately.

TIP

Broccolini (Tenderstem broccoli), pak choi, or other Asian greens in place of the choi sum would work well in this stir-fry.

Greek spinach and feta pie

MEAT-FREE | PREP + COOK TIME **30 MINUTES** | SERVES **1**

The amount of filling will look like quite a lot, but don't be daunted. Keep in mind that the spinach will wilt during cooking, reducing the volume considerably. Double the recipe and you can reheat the pie in a microwave for lunch the next day.

½ cup (120g) fresh firm ricotta

50g feta, crumbled

1 tsp dried oregano

1 spring onion, thinly sliced

1 tbsp finely chopped pitted kalamata olives

40g baby spinach leaves, thinly sliced

¼ cup (10g) coarsely chopped fresh dill

1 egg, lightly beaten

freshly ground black pepper

1 puff pastry sheet (thawed if frozen)

¼ cup (70g) Greek-style yogurt

1 small garlic clove, crushed

green salad, to serve

1   Preheat the oven to 220°C (200°C fan/425°F/Gas 7). Line a baking tray with baking parchment.

2   Combine the ricotta, feta, oregano, onion, olives, spinach, and 2 tablespoons of the dill in a small bowl. Add all but 1 teaspoon of the beaten egg, and mix well. Season with black pepper. (Reserve the remaining egg to brush the pastry.)

3   Using a 24cm plate or bowl as a guide, cut out a circle from the pastry. Spoon the ricotta mixture over one half of the pastry, leaving a 2cm border around the edge. Brush the border with the reserved beaten egg. Fold the pastry over to enclose the filling; press the edge together to seal. Brush the top with the remaining beaten egg.

4   Place the pie on the prepared baking tray; bake for 20 minutes or until the pastry is browned.

5   Meanwhile, combine the remaining dill, yogurt, and garlic in a small bowl. Serve the pie with the dill yogurt and a green salad.

TIP

The uncooked pie can be prepared several hours ahead. Store, covered, in the fridge, until needed.

Sesame-crusted chicken with 'quickled' slaw

KID-FRIENDLY | PREP + COOK TIME **25 MINUTES + STANDING** | SERVES **4**

Pickling generally involves quite a bit of waiting, but with our 'quickled' slaw all the waiting is conveniently done while you are preparing the rest of the recipe. With minimum fuss, you've made a crunchy slaw to accompany tender chicken goujons with a crisp coating.

$^2/_3$ cup (100g) plain flour

2 eggs

1 cup (75g) panko breadcrumbs

$^1/_4$ cup (40g) white sesame seeds

$^1/_4$ cup (50g) black sesame seeds

12 chicken mini breast fillets (900g)

vegetable oil for shallow-frying

salt and freshly ground black pepper

1 lime, halved, to serve

micro herbs, to serve (optional)

'quickled' slaw

1 cucumber (130g)

400g baby carrots, trimmed

$^1/_4$ small red cabbage (300g)

$^1/_2$ cup (125ml) white wine vinegar

1 tbsp caster sugar

$^1/_2$ tsp sea salt flakes

lime mayonnaise

1 cup (300g) Japanese mayonnaise

2 tsp finely grated lime zest

1 tbsp lime juice

1 To make the 'quickled' slaw, using a vegetable peeler, mandolin, or V-slicer, cut the cucumber and carrots lengthways into long, thin ribbons. Finely shred the cabbage. Combine the vegetables with the remaining ingredients in a large glass or ceramic (non-reactive) bowl; allow to stand for 15 minutes. Drain.

2 Meanwhile, to make the lime mayonnaise, combine the ingredients in a small bowl; season with salt and pepper to taste.

3 Put the flour in a shallow bowl; season with salt and pepper to taste. In another shallow bowl, lightly beat the eggs. Put the breadcrumbs and white and black sesame seeds in a third shallow bowl; toss to combine. Coat the chicken mini fillets in the flour; dip in the beaten egg, allowing any excess to drip off, then coat in the breadcrumb mixture.

4 Heat 1cm vegetable oil in a large frying pan over a medium heat. Shallow-fry the chicken, in batches and turning frequently, for $3^1/_2$ minutes or until golden and cooked through. Remove from the pan with a slotted spoon; drain on kitchen paper.

5 Serve the chicken with the slaw, mayonnaise, and lime halves for squeezing over, sprinkled with micro herbs, if you like.

Honey-lemon prawn stir-fry

ONE-POT | PREP + COOK TIME **25 MINUTES** | SERVES **4**

For such a seemingly uncomplicated way of getting meals to the table fast, stir-fries can offer outsize rewards in terms of flavour and freshness to relish and enjoy. If you would like to serve this stir-fry as part of a banquet, pair it with the Vietnamese chicken salad on page 44.

1 tsp sesame seeds

2 tbsp vegetable oil

1kg uncooked medium prawns, shelled, deveined, tails intact

1 large onion (200g), cut into thin wedges

1/2 medium wombok (Chinese leaves) (500g), coarsely chopped

1 large carrot (180g), julienned

1/3 cup (80ml) lemon juice

2 tbsp runny honey

20g piece of fresh root ginger, julienned

450g microwave or instant jasmine rice (see tips)

4 spring onions, thinly sliced

1/4 cup (10g) firmly packed coriander leaves

salt and freshly ground black pepper

1 Toast the sesame seeds in a heated wok until lightly browned; remove from the wok. Set aside.

2 Heat 1 tablespoon of the vegetable oil in the wok over a high heat; stir-fry the prawns for 2 minutes or until the prawns change colour. Remove from the wok and set aside.

3 Heat the remaining 1 tablespoon vegetable oil in the wok over a medium-high heat; stir-fry the onion for 3 minutes or until tender. Return the prawns to the wok with the wombok, carrot, lemon juice, honey, and ginger; stir-fry until hot. Season with salt and pepper to taste.

4 Meanwhile, heat the jasmine rice according to the packet directions.

5 Serve the stir-fry with the rice, sprinkled with the toasted sesame seeds, spring onions, and coriander.

TIPS

- To save time, buy already shelled and deveined prawns from your fishmonger; you will need 500g.
- Have everything prepared before you start to cook.
- Use brown rice instead of jasmine, if you like.
- If you prefer to cook your own rice instead of using precooked, you will need to do this before starting the stir-fry; allow for the extra cooking time.
- If using rice you have already cooked and cooled, always ensure it is piping hot after reheating.

Butternut squash samosa fritters

MEAT-FREE | PREP + COOK TIME **30 MINUTES** | SERVES **2**

Use ready-chopped butternut squash, available from supermarkets and some greengrocers, to save time. You could also microwave the squash. The mixture is quite soft so, if time permits, place the patties in the freezer for 10 minutes, to firm before cooking.

200g butternut squash, coarsely chopped

125g microwave or instant brown rice

$1/4$ cup (30g) frozen garden peas

1 small carrot (70g), coarsely grated

2 tsp curry powder

1 tsp finely grated fresh root ginger

$1/3$ cup (25g) dried breadcrumbs

2 tbsp vegetable oil

salt and freshly ground black pepper

to serve

$1/3$ cup (95g) Greek-style yogurt

2 tbsp hot lime pickle

2 tbsp fresh mint leaves

1   Cook the pumpkin in a medium saucepan of boiling water until tender; drain. Return to the pan, and mash until smooth. Stir the unheated rice, peas, carrot, curry powder, ginger, and breadcrumbs into the mashed pumpkin. Season with salt and pepper to taste.

2   Using oiled hands, form the mixture into 6 patties of about $1/4$ cup each. Heat the vegetable oil in a large frying pan over a medium heat. Cook the patties, in batches, for 2 minutes on each side or until golden. Serve with the yogurt, pickle, and mint leaves. Accompany with a spinach and tomato salad, if you like.

TIP

A condiment made with limes and a characteristic blend of aromatic spices, lime pickle is an Indian speciality that adds a hot and spicy tang to meals.

Fast pasta

Dried pasta, in its many shapes and sizes, is an ideal store-cupboard standby. Ready-made fresh filled pasta is also great for making a speedy, nutritious meal with the addition of just a few ingredients. Remember to keep them on hand in your cupboard or on your shopping list.

Mediterranean mac and cheese

PREP TIME + COOK TIME **35 MINUTES** | SERVES **4**

Cook 375g dried elbow macaroni in a large saucepan of boiling salted water until tender; drain. Meanwhile, melt 60g butter in a large saucepan over a medium heat. Add $1/3$ cup (50g) plain flour; cook, stirring, for 2 minutes or until the mixture bubbles and thickens. Gradually stir in 3 cups (750ml) milk. Add $1/3$ cup (80ml) tomato purée; stir until the sauce boils and thickens. Preheat the grill to high. Stir the pasta, a drained 320g jar antipasto vegetables, and $1/3$ cup (20g) finely chopped chives into the sauce. Put in a deep 2-litre (8-cup) ovenproof dish. Sprinkle with 1 cup (125g) grated mozzarella, $1/2$ cup (50g) grated Cheddar, and 2–3 tablespoons grated Parmesan. Grill until the cheese is melted and golden.

Butternut squash, spinach, and ricotta agnolotti

PREP TIME **25 MINUTES** | SERVES **4**

Cook 625g fresh ricotta and spinach agnolotti in a large saucepan of boiling salted water; drain. Melt 50g butter in the same, cleaned pan over a medium heat; cook 1 bunch of trimmed and finely shredded spinach with 1 teaspoon ground cinnamon until wilted. Remove from the pan. Add 1kg canned butternut squash soup to the pan, bring to the boil; continue boiling for 2 minutes. Add $1/2$ cup (125ml) single cream, spinach, and agnolotti; stir until well combined and heated through. Remove from the heat. Allow to stand for 5 minutes before serving. Season with salt and pepper. Serve the agnolotti topped with 100g crumbled fresh ricotta and fresh flat-leaf parsley leaves.

Chicken pesto pasta with tomatoes

PREP TIME + COOK TIME **25 MINUTES** | SERVES **4**

Preheat the grill to a high heat. Put 250g cherry vine tomatoes with stems attached on a baking tray. Drizzle with 1 teaspoon balsamic glaze; grill for 10 minutes or until the tomato skins begin to split. Meanwhile, cook 375g dried penne pasta in a large saucepan of boiling salted water until tender; drain, reserving $1/3$ cup (80ml) of the cooking liquid. Return the pasta to the pan with $1/3$ cup (80ml) basil pesto, 2 cups (350g) shredded roast chicken, tomatoes, and reserved cooking liquid. Stir gently over a low heat until heated through. Serve sprinkled with 2 tablespoons finely grated Parmesan and some micro basil.

Turkey ragù

PREP TIME **30 MINUTES** | SERVES **4**

Cook 375g fresh or dried fettuccine in a large saucepan of boiling salted water until just tender; drain. Meanwhile, heat 1 tablespoon olive oil in a large frying pan over a high heat; cook 1 finely chopped onion and 2 crushed garlic cloves, stirring, for 3 minutes until soft. Add 1 finely chopped carrot and 1 finely chopped celery stick; cook, stirring, for 5 minutes until just tender. Add 500g minced turkey; cook, stirring, until it changes colour. Add 2 cups (500ml) passata and $1/2$ cup (125ml) chicken stock; bring to the boil. Reduce the heat; simmer for 15 minutes or until the mixture thickens slightly. Add $1/2$ cup (75g) frozen peas; heat through. Season with salt and freshly ground black pepper to taste. Serve the pasta topped with the turkey ragù and $1/3$ cup (25g) shaved Parmesan.

Chana dhal with chutney yogurt

MEAT-FREE | PREP + COOK TIME **30 MINUTES** | SERVES **4**

Chana dal the dried pulse is split chickpeas, but here whole chickpeas are used for a
chunkier, more stew-like texture to the dhal itself. Batch-cook by doubling the recipe, so you
can take the following night off from cooking or take the leftovers to work for lunch.

1 tbsp groundnut oil

1 large onion (200g), thinly sliced

1½ tsp finely grated fresh root ginger

2 tsp light soft brown sugar

⅓ cup (75g) korma paste

1 tsp ground cumin

1 tsp ground turmeric

1 tsp sweet paprika

400g can diced tomatoes

250g cherry tomatoes

1 cup (250ml) coconut milk

400g can brown lentils, drained, rinsed

400g can chickpeas, drained, rinsed

a few sprigs of coriander, to serve

roti bread, warmed, to serve

chutney yogurt

⅔ cup (190g) Greek-style yogurt

1 tbsp mango chutney

1 Heat the groundnut oil in a large saucepan over a medium heat.
Add the onion, ginger, and brown sugar; cook, stirring, for 5 minutes
or until soft. Next, add the korma paste and spices; cook, stirring, for
1 minute or until fragrant.

2 Add the canned tomatoes, cherry tomatoes, 1 cup (250ml) water, coconut
milk, lentils, and chickpeas to the pan; bring to the boil. Reduce the heat,
and simmer for 10 minutes or until the mixture has thickened slightly.

3 Meanwhile, to make the chutney yogurt, swirl together the yogurt and
mango chutney in a small bowl.

4 Serve the dhal sprinkled with coriander, dollops of chutney yogurt,
and warm roti bread.

TIP

Freeze individual portions of dhal in airtight
containers for up to 1 month. Thaw the dhal
overnight in the fridge. If taking it to work,
reheat the thawed dhal in the microwave
just before eating.

Chilli and chicken tostada

CHEAT EAT | PREP + COOK TIME **25 MINUTES** | SERVES **2**

A speciality of Mexico and elsewhere in Latin America, tostadas vary in fillings, but all feature a bowl-shaped fried or toasted tortilla. This recipe can easily be doubled. For a vegetarian version, replace the chicken in step 3 with a 400g can rinsed, drained kidney beans.

2 jumbo tortillas or wraps

2 tbsp vegetable oil, plus extra for brushing

2¹/₂ tbsp finely chopped chipotle chilli in adobo sauce

4 chicken thigh fillets (800g), trimmed

1 corn cob (400g)

4 large cherry tomatoes (50g), seeded, finely diced

1 lime, quartered

2 tbsp finely chopped coriander, plus extra ¹/₃ cup (10g) coriander sprigs

250g packet microwave or instant brown rice

¹/₂ cup (40g) thinly sliced red cabbage

1 tbsp soured cream

salt and freshly ground black pepper

1 Preheat the oven to 180°C (160°C fan/350°F/Gas 4).

2 Cut a wedge (8cm at its top) from each of the tortillas. Brush the tortillas and wedges on both sides with the extra vegetable oil. Place each tortilla in an ovenproof bowl, slightly overlapping the cut edges of the tortillas to form the shape of a bowl. Bake in the oven for 6 minutes. Carefully transfer the tortillas, domed side up, to a small baking tray with the tortilla wedges; bake for a further 6 minutes or until golden. The tortilla bowls (tostadas) and tortilla wedges will crisp as they cool.

3 Meanwhile, combine half of the chipotle chilli and the 2 tablespoons vegetable oil in a small bowl; season with salt to taste. Add the chicken; turn to coat in the mixture.

4 Heat a frying pan over a high heat. Cook the chicken for 4 minutes on each side or until cooked through, adding the corn to the pan during the last 4 minutes of cooking time. Rest the chicken for 5 minutes, then thinly slice the chicken and the corn kernels from the cob.

5 Meanwhile, to make the salsa, combine the remaining chipotle chilli, tomatoes, juice of 2 of the lime wedges, and the 2 tablespoons chopped coriander in a bowl. Season with salt and pepper to taste.

6 Heat the rice according to the packet instructions. Divide the warmed rice among the tostadas; top with the chicken, corn kernels, extra coriander sprigs, red cabbage, and salsa. Serve with the soured cream and the remaining lime wedges for squeezing over.

TIPS

- Chipotle in adobo is a hot, smoky-flavoured Mexican sauce made from chipotles (smoke-dried jalapeno chillies). It is available from supermarkets.
- Store any leftover chipotle in a small screw-top jar in the fridge for up to 1 month.
- To make a chicken burrito, warm the tortillas and wrap around the filling ingredients.

Crisp fish with buckwheat salad

GLUTEN-FREE/HEALTHY CHOICE | PREP + COOK TIME **30 MINUTES** | SERVES **4**

Despite its name, buckwheat is unrelated to wheat and is in fact a seed, making it an ideal choice for gluten-free diets. Buckwheat is processed into groats that are cooked in a similar way to rice; it is also ground as a flour.

2 tbsp groundnut oil

¼ cup (45g) rice flour

4 x 200g firm white fish fillets, skin on

salt and freshly ground black pepper

buckwheat salad

100g snow peas (mangetout), trimmed

1 tbsp groundnut oil

1 tbsp light soy sauce

1 tsp finely grated fresh root ginger

2 tbsp lime juice

2 tsp light soft brown sugar

1 carrot (120g), julienned

1 cup (80g) beansprouts, trimmed

⅓ cup (65g) roasted buckwheat kernels (see tip)

1 cup (30g) coriander leaves

1 To make the buckwheat salad, boil, steam, or microwave the snow peas until tender; drain. Rinse under cold water; drain. Put the groundnut oil, soy sauce, ginger, lime juice, and brown sugar in a large bowl; whisk well. Add the snow peas and the remaining ingredients; toss gently. Season with salt and pepper to taste.

2 Heat the oil in a large frying pan over a medium heat. Put the rice flour in a shallow bowl; season with salt and pepper to taste. Coat the fish in flour; shake off any excess. Cook the fish, skin-side down, for 5 minutes or until golden and crisp; turn and cook for a further 5 minutes or until just cooked through.

3 Serve the fish with the buckwheat salad.

TIP

If you can't find roasted buckwheat kernels, roast the kernels in the oven at 180°C (160°C fan/350°F/Gas 4) for about 5 minutes; cool before using.

Minestrone with beef ravioli

CHEAP EAT/KID-FRIENDLY | PREP + COOK TIME **25 MINUTES** | SERVES **2**

Fresh ravioli is available from the refrigerated section of most supermarkets. For a vegetarian minestrone, use spinach and ricotta ravioli instead. And if you don't have chilli oil, sprinkle the soup with a pinch of dried chilli flakes for a touch of heat.

2 tsp extra virgin olive oil

½ small onion (40g), finely chopped

1 garlic clove, crushed

2 tsp finely chopped rosemary leaves

1 small carrot (70g), finely chopped

1 trimmed celery stick (100g), finely chopped

400g can diced tomatoes

2 cups (500ml) vegetable stock

1 tsp caster sugar

150g fresh beef ravioli

2 tbsp shaved Parmesan

1 tsp chilli oil

1 tbsp flat-leaf parsley leaves

salt and freshly ground black pepper

crusty bread, to serve

1 Heat the oil in a medium saucepan over a medium heat. Cook the onion, garlic, rosemary, carrot, and celery for 5 minutes or until softened.

2 Add the tomatoes, stock, and sugar; season with salt and pepper to taste. Bring to the boil; cook for 5 minutes. Add the ravioli, cook for 5 minutes or until the ravioli is tender.

3 Divide the soup and ravioli evenly between 2 serving bowls. Top with the Parmesan, drizzle with the chilli oil, and scatter over the parsley. Serve accompanied by the crusty bread.

TIP

If freezing the soup to use later, don't add the ravioli. Make the soup, then cool and store in a freezerproof container. Thaw and reheat when needed, then add the ravioli as at step 2, and continue with the recipe.

Rigatoni with arrabbiata and chorizo sauce

KID-FRIENDLY | PREP + COOK TIME **25 MINUTES** | SERVES **4**

'Arrabbiata' means angry in Italian, and here this tomato sauce with a chilli kick is combined with spicy chorizo to make a tasty weeknight standard. There's no need to add oil to the frying pan when cooking the chorizo, as sufficient fat will be released during cooking.

500g dried penne or rigatoni pasta

300g cured chorizo, thinly sliced

2 tbsp extra virgin olive oil

1 large onion (200g), finely chopped

1 tsp dried chilli flakes

3 garlic cloves, crushed

700ml bottled passata

$^1\!/_2$ tsp light soft brown sugar

$^1\!/_2$ cup (15g) coarsely chopped flat-leaf parsley

$^2\!/_3$ cup (70g) finely grated Parmesan

salt

1 Cook the pasta in a large saucepan of boiling water until almost tender; drain. Return to the pan and set aside.

2 Meanwhile, cook the chorizo in a large frying pan over a medium-high heat, turning occasionally, for 2 minutes or until the chorizo is browned. Remove from the pan; set aside to drain on kitchen paper.

3 Add the olive oil to the same frying pan; cook the onion, chilli, and garlic, stirring, for 3 minutes or until the onion softens. Add the passata, sugar, and 1 cup (250ml) water. Bring to the boil. Reduce the heat to low; simmer, stirring occasionally, for 7 minutes or until the sauce has thickened slightly. Add the chorizo; stir to combine. Cook for 2 minutes or until heated through. Season with salt to taste.

4 Add the arrabbiata sauce and the parsley to the cooked pasta in the pan; stir over a medium heat until heated through. Stir in the Parmesan.

Five-spice pork with almonds

HEALTHY CHOICE | PREP + COOK TIME **30 MINUTES** | SERVES **4**

Five-spice powder is based on the Chinese philosophy of balancing the five main flavours of sweet, sour, salt, bitter, and pungent, which correspond with the five elements of earth, wood, water, fire, and metal. The mix contains star anise, fennel seeds, Sichuan pepper, cloves, and cinnamon.

750g pork fillets, thinly sliced

1 tsp garam masala

2 tsp Chinese five-spice powder

1 tbsp groundnut oil

1 carrot (120g), julienned

2 garlic cloves, crushed

1 tbsp finely grated fresh root ginger

4 baby pak choi (600g), halved lengthways

1 tbsp sweet chilli sauce

1/4 cup (60ml) oyster sauce

2 tbsp lime juice

2 tbsp hot water

100g snow peas (mangetout), trimmed

1 cup (80g) beansprouts

1/3 cup (55g) blanched almonds, roasted, coarsely chopped

1 lime (65g), cut into wedges

rice noodles or steamed rice, to serve

1 Combine the pork and spices in a large bowl; mix well.

2 Heat half of the groundnut oil in a wok over a high heat; stir-fry the pork mixture, in batches, for 2–3 minutes until the pork is browned and tender. Remove from the wok and set aside.

3 Heat the remaining groundnut oil in the wok; add the carrot, garlic, and ginger. Stir-fry for 2 minutes, then add the pak choi, sweet chilli sauce, oyster sauce, lime juice, and 2 tablespoons hot water; stir-fry for 4 minutes or until the pak choi is tender.

4 Return the pork to the wok with the snow peas; stir-fry until heated through. Serve topped with the beansprouts and almonds, and with the lime wedges for squeezing over. Accompany with rice noodles or steamed rice.

TIPS

- You can substitute the pork with chicken, lamb, or beef, if you like.
- For a nut-free version, use vegetable oil instead of groundnut oil, and replace the almonds with Asian fried shallots.

Spiced steaks with grilled aubergine salad

HEALTHY CHOICE | PREP + COOK TIME **15 MINUTES** | SERVES **2**

Pomegranate molasses, made by boiling down pomegranate juice into a thick syrup, has long been used as a seasoning in Persian and other Middle Eastern cuisines. Here, it provides a pleasant sweet–tart tang for the dressing used for the aubergine salad.

2 tbsp extra virgin olive oil

1 tsp ground allspice

2 aubergines (200g), halved lengthways

2 x 200g beef ribeye steaks

2 small tomatoes (180g), roughly chopped

2 spring onions, thinly sliced

¼ cup (5g) mint leaves

2 tsp pomegranate molasses

salt and freshly ground black pepper

1 Heat a ridged cast-iron grill pan over a medium-high heat. Put 1 tablespoon of the olive oil and the allspice in a medium bowl. Season with salt and pepper to taste. Toss the aubergines in the mixture to coat; shake off any excess. Next, toss the steaks in the mixture to coat.

2 Cook the steaks for 2 minutes on each side for medium-rare or until cooked to your liking. Remove, cover loosely with foil, and allow to rest for 5 minutes. Add the aubergine to the same pan; cook for 2 minutes on each side or until softened.

3 Meanwhile, divide the tomato, spring onion, and mint between 2 serving plates. Whisk together the remaining 1 tablespoon olive oil and the pomegranate molasses in a small bowl until combined; season with salt and pepper to taste.

4 Slice the steaks and aubergine, and transfer to the serving plates. Drizzle with the pomegranate dressing to serve.

TIPS

- Accompany with wholegrain couscous or flatbread, if you like.
- You can use lamb sirloin chops in place of the beef.

SOMETHING SPECIAL

For fast inspiration for that indefinable element to turn a meal into an occasion, from celebratory meals to dinner parties and informal entertaining, here are your answers.

Beetroot tartare with whipped feta

MEAT-FREE | PREP + COOK TIME **20 MINUTES + REFRIGERATION** | SERVES **8**

This is the perfect easy starter to whip up for entertaining, as it can also be made ahead to the end of step 3 and refrigerated a day ahead. It looks and tastes impressive, too, with its ruby-red beetroot and a balance of sweet, salty, sour, and nutty crunch to tempt the palate.

200g goat's milk feta

1/3 cup (80g) soured cream

1/4 cup (60ml) extra virgin olive oil

1kg cooked beetroot

1/2 cup (90g) drained cornichons

1 tbsp horseradish cream

3 tsp vegetarian Worcestershire sauce

2 tsp Dijon mustard

1 tbsp baby capers in vinegar, chopped

1 tsp caper pickling liquid

2 tbsp pumpkin seeds

salt and freshly ground black pepper

micro rocket, to serve

crispbreads or sliced baguette, to serve

1 To make the whipped feta, process the feta, soured cream, and 1 tablespoon of the olive oil for 3 minutes or until smooth. Stop the processor and scrape down the side of the bowl with a spatula twice during processing. Transfer to a serving bowl; season with salt and pepper to taste. Cover and refrigerate for 15 minutes to thicken.

2 Cut the beetroot into 1cm cubes. Finely chop half of the cornichons. Transfer the beetroot and chopped cornichons to a medium bowl; stir in the remaining olive oil, horseradish cream, Worcestershire sauce, Dijon mustard, capers, and caper pickling liquid. Season with salt and pepper to taste.

3 Spoon the beetroot mixture onto a large plate or bowl; sprinkle with the pumpkin seeds and micro rocket. Serve the tartare with the whipped feta, remaining cornichons, and crispbreads.

TIP

Spread the whipped feta onto the crispbread first, then top with the beetroot tartare to prevent the beetroot tartare falling off the bread.

Jerk salmon with yogurt potatoes

HEALTHY CHOICE | PREP + COOK TIME **20 MINUTES** | SERVES **2**

'Jerk' is the name of the Jamaican dry or wet spice rub used to season fish and chicken; it is also the name of the cooking method, where traditionally the meat is slow-cooked over a fire. Chilli and allspice are the two defining spices in the rub, and both feature here.

8 baby new potatoes (320g), thickly sliced

1/3 cup (10g) firmly packed flat-leaf parsley

1/3 cup (15g) firmly packed coriander

1 tsp freshly ground black pepper

1 tsp dried chilli flakes

1 tsp ground allspice

2 garlic cloves, crushed

2 tsp finely grated fresh root ginger

1/4 cup (60ml) lime juice

1/4 cup (60ml) extra virgin olive oil

2 x 200g skinless salmon fillets

1/4 cup (70g) Greek-style yogurt

2 shallots (50g), finely chopped

salt

1   Boil, steam, or microwave the potato until tender; cover to keep warm.

2   Reserve 1 tablespoon each of the parsley and coriander. Process the remaining herbs with the black pepper, chilli flakes, allspice, garlic, ginger, lime juice, and olive oil; season with salt to taste.

3   Pour half of the herb mixture over the salmon in a medium bowl; allow to stand for 5 minutes.

4   Heat a medium non-stick frying pan over a medium heat. Add the undrained salmon; cook, for 2 minutes on each side or until just cooked through (be careful not to overcook).

5   Combine the potato with the yogurt, shallot, and remaining herb mixture. Serve topped with the salmon, and sprinkled with the reserved parsley and coriander.

TIPS

- You will need 1 lime for this recipe. To help with juicing, roll the lime firmly on a hard surface first.
- You can substitute the ground allspice with 1/2 teaspoon ground cinnamon and 1/4 teaspoon each of ground cloves and nutmeg.

Barbecued steak with anchovy vinaigrette

HEALTHY CHOICE | PREP + COOK TIME **30 MINUTES + STANDING** | SERVES **6**

This flavoursome steak is marinated first, before being cooked at a high temperature and doused in a bold vinaigrette to improve its flavour even further. Accompany with a serving of rocket, baby spinach, or watercress.

1.2kg skirt steak

2 tbsp extra virgin olive oil

2 tsp garlic powder

2 tsp light soft brown sugar

1½ tsp sea salt flakes

1 tsp freshly ground black pepper

250g cherry vine tomatoes

anchovy vinaigrette

⅓ cup (80ml) extra virgin olive oil

1 shallot, finely chopped

8 anchovy fillets (20g), finely chopped

2 long red chillies, seeded, finely chopped

1 tbsp thyme leaves, finely chopped

2 tsp each of chopped fresh rosemary and oregano

3 garlic cloves, peeled

2 tsp finely grated lemon zest

2 tbsp lemon juice

1 tbsp red wine vinegar

salt and freshly ground black pepper

1 To make the anchovy vinaigrette, heat the olive oil in a small saucepan over a medium heat. Cook the shallot for 3 minutes or until softened. Add the anchovies and chillies; cook for 1 minute or until the anchovy is soft. Transfer to a heatproof bowl; stir in the herbs. Grate the garlic into the hot anchovy mixture using a fine grater or Microplane. Allow to cool. Stir in the lemon zest, lemon juice, and red wine vinegar. Season with salt and pepper to taste.

2 Meanwhile, pat dry the steak with kitchen paper. Combine the oil, garlic powder, brown sugar, sea salt, and black pepper in a large stainless-steel or glass bowl. Add the steak to the bowl; rub the oil mixture all over the steak until evenly coated. Allow to stand at room temperature for 20 minutes.

3 Preheat a barbecue (or grill plate or ridged cast-iron grill pan) to a high heat. Cook the steak for 4 minutes on each side for medium, or until grill marks appear and the steak is cooked to your liking (see tip). Transfer to a tray, cover loosely with foil, and allow to rest for at least 10 minutes. Barbecue the whole tomatoes for 2 minutes or until softened slightly. Season with salt and pepper to taste.

4 Slice the steak; drizzle with the anchovy vinaigrette. Serve with the barbecued tomatoes.

TIPS

• Skirt is a less expensive steak cut with great flavour, though a little chewy. It benefits from either long, slow cooking or quick searing. Bring to room temperature first, then rest well before serving.

• You can also use rump, sirloin, ribeye, or eye fillet. Cook for 4 minutes on each side for a 2cm thick steak, and about 10 minutes each side for a 5cm one.

Whipped edamame with crisp rice paper crackers

MEAT-FREE | PREP + COOK TIME **30 MINUTES** | SERVES **8**

This dip is a good choice for entertaining. The whipped edamame can be made up to 4 hours ahead and refrigerated. The rice paper crackers can be fried up to 2 hours ahead; store between sheets of kitchen paper in an airtight container until needed.

4 cups (800g) frozen shelled edamame (see tips)

$^1/_3$ cup (80ml) groundnut oil, plus extra for shallow-frying

2 tbsp sesame oil

$^1/_3$ cup (80ml) mirin

$^1/_3$ cup (80ml) rice wine vinegar

$^1/_4$ cup (75g) dashi miso paste (see tips)

2 tbsp lemon juice

1 tbsp Japanese mayonnaise

16 x 16cm round rice paper wrappers (80g)

1 tsp black sesame seeds (see tips)

micro coriander, to serve

$^1/_3$ cup (95g) pink pickled ginger, drained

1 Cook the edamame in a large saucepan of boiling water for 5 minutes or until tender; drain. Refresh in a bowl of iced water; drain.

2 Process the edamame with the $^1/_3$ cup (80ml) groundnut oil, sesame oil, mirin, rice wine vinegar, dashi miso paste, lemon juice, mayonnaise, and $^1/_3$ cup (80ml) water for 3 minutes or until pale and smooth; stop the processor and scrape the side occasionally. Transfer to a bowl; cover and set aside until needed.

3 Meanwhile, fill a large saucepan one-third full with the extra groundnut oil; heat to 180°C/350°F (or until a cube of bread dropped into the oil turns golden in 15 seconds). Deep-fry 1 rice paper round at a time for 5 seconds or until puffed. Drain on kitchen paper.

4 Sprinkle the whipped edamame with the sesame seeds and micro coriander. Serve with the pickled ginger and rice paper crackers.

TIPS

- Fresh or frozen shelled edamame are available from supermarkets and Asian food stores. If using edamame in the shell, you will need about 2kg.
- Look for dashi miso paste at Asian grocers or in the international section of supermarkets.
- Black sesame seeds are available from Asian and Middle Eastern food stores. If unavailable, top with well-toasted white sesame seeds.

Pistachio pilaf with chargrilled lamb

GLUTEN-FREE | PREP + COOK TIME **30 MINUTES** | SERVES **6**

Lamb cutlets are sweet and succulent, cut as they are from ribs of lamb, and so really don't need much more than a simple seasoning of salt and pepper, paired with quick grilling over not too high a heat, to be at their most tender and juicy.

30g butter, chopped

1 onion (150g), finely chopped

1 tbsp finely chopped fresh root ginger

1 cinnamon stick

4 green cardamom pods, cracked

$\frac{1}{2}$ tsp ground turmeric

$\frac{1}{4}$ cup (6g) loosely packed curry leaves

2 cups (400g) basmati rice

3 cups (750ml) gluten-free chicken stock or water

12 large French-trimmed lamb cutlets (600g)

2 tbsp extra virgin olive oil

2 cups (20g) flat-leaf parsley, coarsely torn

2 cups (20g) mint, coarsely torn

$\frac{1}{3}$ cup (45g) pistachios, coarsely chopped

$\frac{1}{3}$ cup (55g) dry-roasted almonds, coarsely chopped

2 tbsp currants

2 tbsp lemon juice

salt and freshly ground black pepper

lemon wedges, to serve

Greek-style yogurt, to serve

1 Heat the butter in a large saucepan over a medium-high heat. Add the onion; cook, stirring, for 5 minutes or until softened. Next, add the ginger, spices, curry leaves, and basmati rice; stir to combine. Pour in the chicken stock; bring to the boil. Reduce to the lowest heat; cook, covered, for 10 minutes or until most of the liquid is absorbed. Allow to stand, covered, for 5 minutes.

2 Meanwhile, preheat a grill plate (or ridged cast-iron grill pan or barbecue) to a medium-high heat. Drizzle the lamb with the olive oil; season with salt and pepper to taste. Cook the lamb for $3\frac{1}{2}$ minutes on each side for medium, or until cooked to your liking.

3 Stir the parsley, mint, pistachios, almonds, currants, and lemon juice into the rice pilaf; season with salt and pepper to taste. Serve the pilaf with the lamb, lemon wedges for squeezing over, and yogurt.

TIPS

- 'French-trimmed' refers to the process of cleaning the bone ends of the cutlets of fat and sinew for a clean presentation.
- To tear herbs coarsely, simply use your hands to tear them straight from the bunch. Alternatively, run a knife over the whole bunch, coarsely chopping both leaves and stems at the same time.

Snapper in banana leaves with Thai herb salad

HEALTHY CHOICE | PREP + COOK TIME **30 MINUTES + STANDING** | SERVES **4**

Wrapping fish in banana leaves helps to keep it moist and holds in the flavours of the other ingredients so that they permeate the whole fish. This technique for marinating fish and meat is found across Southeast Asia, as well as in other tropical regions of the world.

2 tbsp Thai red curry paste

4 garlic cloves, crushed

2 makrut lime leaves, finely chopped

$^{1}/_{3}$ cup (80ml) lime juice

2 tbsp fish sauce

$^{1}/_{2}$ cup (135g) finely grated palm sugar

1.5kg whole snapper or mackerel, cleaned

8 banana leaves (see tips)

Thai herb salad

200g cherry tomatoes, halved

2 spring onions, thinly sliced

1 cup (30g) coriander leaves

$^{1}/_{2}$ cup (15g) Thai basil leaves

$^{1}/_{2}$ cup (10g) mint leaves

2 tbsp lime juice

2 tbsp fish sauce

1 tbsp groundnut oil

$^{1}/_{3}$ cup (90g) finely grated palm sugar

1 Heat the red curry paste in a small saucepan for 2 minutes or until fragrant. Remove from the heat; stir in the garlic, lime leaves, lime juice, fish sauce, and palm sugar until combined.

2 Rinse the fish; pat dry with kitchen paper. Cut diagonal slashes in the fish 2cm apart on both sides.

3 Spoon half of the curry paste mixture over both sides of the fish; reserve the remaining paste mixture to serve. Wrap the fish in the banana leaves; secure with kitchen string or toothpicks (cocktail sticks).

4 Preheat a barbecue (or grill plate) to a high heat. Cook the fish for 10 minutes on each side. Allow to stand for 5 minutes to finish cooking, before opening the leaves.

5 Meanwhile, to make the Thai herb salad, put the tomatoes, spring onions, and herbs in a bowl. Combine the remaining ingredients in a jug or bowl. Just before serving, pour the dressing over the salad; toss to combine.

6 Open the banana-leaf parcel; discard the toothpicks (if using). Serve the fish topped with the Thai herb salad and drizzled with the reserved red curry paste mixture.

TIPS

• If you can't source banana leaves, top 2 large sheets of foil with baking parchment. Place the fish on 1 layered sheet of foil and top with the second stack, baking-parchment-side down; fold in the edges several times to create a secure parcel.

• Prop up the fish tail with a ball of foil to prevent it burning on the barbecue or grill plate. The fish can be prepared to the end of step 3 up to 3 hours ahead; refrigerate until ready to cook.

Haloumi skewers with blackberry dressing

GLUTEN-FREE | PREP + COOK TIME **30 MINUTES** | MAKES **8**

The semi-hard cheese haloumi has a high melting point, making it ideal for grilling.
It's important to thread same-sized pieces of the haloumi onto the same skewers, so that
all pieces of the haloumi touch the grill during cooking.

8 prosciutto slices (120g)

350g haloumi, cut into 24 pieces (see tips)

2 tbsp extra virgin olive oil

1 red chicory (125g), sliced (see tips)

1 white chicory (125g), sliced

¼ cup (35g) skinless toasted hazelnuts, chopped

¼ cup (7g) small mint leaves

blackberry dressing

⅓ cup (95g) Greek-style yogurt

125g blackberries

1 tbsp sherry vinegar

1 tbsp runny honey

salt and freshly ground black pepper

1 To make the blackberry dressing, blend the ingredients in a small blender until smooth and well combined; season with salt and pepper to taste.

2 Cut the prosciutto into 3 strips lengthways. Roughly fold 8 strips of the prosciutto and thread onto 8 skewers. Thread a piece of haloumi onto skewers; repeat twice with the remaining prosciutto and haloumi. Place the skewers on a plate; brush with the olive oil.

3 Meanwhile, preheat a grill plate (or ridged cast-iron grill pan or barbecue flat plate) to a high heat. Grill the skewers for 1 minute on each side or until the haloumi is well browned.

4 Arrange the chicory and skewers on a plate; drizzle with the blackberry dressing. Serve with the hazelnuts and mint scattered over the top.

TIPS

- Chicory varieties are slightly bitter; use rocket, watercress, or mixed salad leaves instead, if you like.
- If you can't find fresh blackberries, thaw frozen blackberries and pat them dry before using.
- The dressing can be made up to 3 days ahead; refrigerate, covered, until needed.

Pork filet mignon with mushroom sauce

GLUTEN-FREE | PREP + COOK TIME **30 MINUTES** | SERVES **4**

Pork fillet, or tenderloin, is one of the tenderest cuts of pork, as its name implies.
That means it's highly suited to quick cooking methods. And for a speedy salad to accompany
the filet mignon, choose one of the Fast Salads on page 44.

16 fresh sage leaves

4 prosciutto slices (60g)

4 x 250g pork fillets (pork tenderloin)

2 tbsp olive oil

200g thinly sliced chestnut mushrooms

1 small onion (80g), thinly sliced

1 garlic clove, crushed

1½ cups (375ml) gluten-free beef stock

1 tbsp tomato purée

125g frozen chopped spinach

475g ready-made gluten-free
cheesy mashed potato

salt and freshly ground black pepper

1   Place 2 of the sage leaves along each slice of prosciutto. Wrap 1 slice of the prosciutto around each pork fillet; secure in place with toothpicks or cocktail sticks.

2   Preheat an oiled grill plate (or ridged cast-iron grill pan or barbecue) to a medium-high heat. Cook the pork, turning, for 10 minutes or until browned all over and cooked through. Remove from the pan; cover to keep warm.

3   Meanwhile, heat the olive oil in a medium frying pan over a high heat. Cook the remaining sage leaves for 30 seconds or until crisp. Remove from the pan with a slotted spoon; set aside to drain on kitchen paper. Reduce the heat to medium-high. Cook the mushrooms, onion, and garlic in the same pan, stirring occasionally, for 4 minutes or until the mushrooms are golden and tender. Add the stock and tomato purée. Bring to the boil, then reduce the heat. Simmer for 5 minutes or until the sauce thickens slightly.

4   Meanwhile, microwave the spinach on HIGH (100%) for 1 minute or until hot. Place the spinach in a fine sieve; squeeze out the excess water. Heat the mashed potato according to the packet directions. Transfer to a large serving bowl. Stir the spinach through the mash; season with salt and pepper to taste.

5   Thickly slice the pork; sprinkle with the crisp sage leaves. Serve with the mash and the mushroom sauce.

TIP

Pork is a lean cut, so care should be taken not to overcook it or it will be dry.

Thai fish burgers with pickled vegetables

CHEAT EAT | PREP + COOK TIME **30 MINUTES** | SERVES **4**

Pungently aromatic makrut lime leaves add their distinctive flavour to these fishcakes.
To use makrut lime leaves, fold a leaf in half and cut out the tough centre vein. Leftover leaves
will keep in an airtight container in the fridge for 2 weeks or can be frozen for up to 1 month.

2 cucumbers (260g)

1 large carrot (180g)

2 long red chillies, thinly sliced

2 tbsp caster sugar

2 tbsp white vinegar

600g skinless white fish fillets

2 tbsp Thai red curry paste

2 tbsp fish sauce

4 fresh makrut lime leaves, thinly sliced

6 green beans, thinly sliced

1 egg

½ cup (15g) coriander leaves

2 tbsp groundnut or vegetable oil

⅓ cup (80ml) sweet chilli sauce

4 large bread rolls, split horizontally

1 Using a mandolin, V-slicer, or wide vegetable peeler, thinly slice the cucumber and carrot lengthways into long ribbons. Combine the cucumber, carrot, chillies, caster sugar, and white vinegar in a medium bowl. Allow to stand for 10 minutes or until the vegetables have softened, turning every few minutes. Drain.

2 Meanwhile, pulse the fish, red curry paste, fish sauce, lime leaves, green beans, egg, and half of the coriander leaves in a food processor for 1 minute or until smooth. Using oiled hands, shape the mixture into four 12cm patties.

3 Heat the groundnut oil in a large frying pan over a medium heat. Cook the patties for 2 minutes on each side or until cooked through. Drain on kitchen paper.

4 Add the bread rolls, cut-side down, to the same frying pan; cook for 1 minute or until lightly toasted.

5 Sandwich the fish burgers, sweet chilli sauce, pickled vegetables, and remaining coriander in the rolls. Serve immediately.

TIP

Fish patties can be prepared several hours ahead; store, covered, in the fridge until ready to cook.

Cheat's roast lamb dinner

KID-FRIENDLY | PREP + COOK TIME **30 MINUTES** | SERVES **4**

Bangers and mash meets the traditional accompaniment of fresh mint sauce in this cheat's version of a classic lamb roast – meat and three veg has never been so moreish. The mint sauce is simple to put together and beats shop-bought versions hands-down.

8 thick lamb sausages (1.2kg)

800g all-purpose potatoes, peeled, coarsely chopped

500g frozen broad beans

400g baby carrots, trimmed

40g butter

1/2 cup (125ml) hot milk

1/4 cup (7g) small mint leaves

salt and freshly ground black pepper

mint sauce

2 cups (50g) firmly packed mint leaves

2 garlic cloves, quartered

1/2 cup (125ml) olive oil

1/4 cup (60ml) white wine vinegar

1 tbsp caster sugar

1   Heat a ridged cast-iron grill pan (or grill) over a medium-high heat. Cook the sausages, turning, for 8 minutes or until cooked through.

2   Meanwhile, boil, steam, or microwave the potatoes, beans, and carrots separately until tender; drain. Cover the carrots to keep warm. Push the potatoes through a fine sieve into a large bowl; stir in the butter and milk until smooth. Peel the broad beans. Put the beans in a small bowl; crush coarsely with fork. Fold the beans into the potato mixture. Season with salt and pepper to taste; cover to keep warm.

3   To make the mint sauce, blend or process the mint and garlic until smooth. With the motor operating, gradually add the oil, in a thin, steady stream, until the mixture is smooth. Stir in the vinegar and sugar.

4   Serve the sausages with the mint sauce, carrots, and broad bean mash, sprinkled with the mint leaves. Season with salt and pepper to taste.

TIP

Broad beans are available both frozen and fresh from most supermarkets. If you can't find any, use frozen peas in the mash instead.

Sausage and peppers with soft polenta

KID-FRIENDLY | PREP + COOK TIME **30 MINUTES** | SERVES **4**

This is quick winter comfort food at its best and can be made even faster if you would like by swapping out the polenta for a tub of cheesy mash. The creamy, cheesy polenta is well worth the small amount of effort required, though, and the reward is in its eating.

2 tbsp olive oil

6 pork and fennel sausages (400g)

2 large red peppers (700g), thickly sliced

2 large onions (400g), thinly sliced

2 tbsp rosemary leaves

3 garlic cloves, sliced

1 cup (250ml) dry white wine

6 cups (1.5 litres) chicken stock

250g green beans, trimmed

1 cup (170g) instant polenta

1 cup (100g) finely grated Parmesan, plus extra 2 tbsp, to serve

30g butter, chopped

salt and freshly ground black pepper

1 Heat the olive oil in a large, heavy-based frying pan over a high heat. Squeeze the sausage meat directly from the casings, in meatball-sized lumps, into the pan. Cook, turning, for 4 minutes or until browned. Remove the meatballs from the pan; set aside.

2 Reduce the heat to medium. Cook the red peppers, onions, rosemary, and garlic for 5 minutes. Add the meatballs and wine; cook for 1 minute. Add 1 cup (250ml) of the stock and the green beans to the pan; cook, covered, for 10 minutes or until the meatballs are cooked through.

3 Meanwhile, put the remaining 5 cups (1.25 litres) stock in a medium saucepan; bring to the boil. Gradually add the polenta. Reduce the heat to low; cook, stirring, for 5 minutes or until thickened. Remove from the heat, and stir in the 1 cup (80g) Parmesan and the butter; season with salt and pepper to taste.

4 Serve the meatballs with the polenta and green beans, sprinkled with the extra Parmesan.

Salmon with fennel and ruby grapefruit salad

HEALTHY CHOICE | PREP + COOK TIME **30 MINUTES** | SERVES **4**

You can also use a white fish such as mackerel or sea bass for this recipe. The salad, with its balance of bold flavours and textures, acts as a foil to the succulent fish. When segmenting the grapefruit, don't forget to reserve 2 tablespoons of the juice to use in the dressing.

3 baby fennel bulbs (390g), shaved, fronds reserved

2 red grapefruit (700g), segmented, with 2 tbsp juice reserved for the dressing

8 radishes (280g), trimmed, thinly sliced (see tips)

1 small red onion (100g), thinly sliced (see tips)

³/₄ cup (120g) kalamata olives

¹/₄ cup (7g) firmly packed flat-leaf parsley leaves

¹/₄ cup (7g) small mint leaves

1 tbsp lemon juice

2 tbsp extra virgin olive oil

4 x 200g boneless salmon fillets, skin on

30g butter

salt and freshly ground black pepper

citrus dressing

2 tbsp extra virgin olive oil

2 tbsp reserved red grapefruit juice (see above)

1 tbsp lemon juice

1 tsp Dijon mustard

1 To make the citrus dressing, put the ingredients in a small screw-top jar with a tight-fitting lid; shake until well combined. Season with salt and pepper to taste. Set aside.

2 Put the fennel, grapefruit, radishes, onion, olives, parsley, and mint in a large bowl with the lemon juice and 1 tablespoon of the olive oil; toss gently to combine. Season with salt and pepper to taste.

3 Heat the remaining 1 tablespoon olive oil in a large heavy-based frying pan over a high heat. Season the salmon with salt and pepper to taste. Cook the salmon, skin-side down, for 1 minute or until golden brown. Turn over; add the butter to the pan. Cook until the butter turns nut brown. Continue cooking the salmon for a further 30 seconds or until just cooked through.

4 Divide the salad and salmon evenly among 4 serving plates; sprinkle with the reserved fennel fronds. Season with salt and pepper to taste. Drizzle with the citrus dressing, and serve.

TIPS

• Use a mandolin or V-slicer, if you have one, to thinly slice the fennel, radishes, and onion.

• The dressing can be made and refrigerated in the jar up to 2 days ahead.

Greek pork skewers with crushed white beans

KID-FRIENDLY | PREP + COOK TIME **30 MINUTES** | SERVES **4**

Souvlaki, skewers of grilled meat and sometimes vegetables usually cooked over a spit, is almost an art form in Greece and a very popular street food. The usual choice of meat is pork, as in the skewers here, and they are accompanied by another Greek standard, a chunky white bean dip made with cannellini or white kidney beans.

¹/₄ cup (60ml) extra virgin olive oil

1 onion (150g), thinly sliced

3 garlic cloves, 1 thinly sliced and 2 halved

¹/₂ cup (125ml) dry white wine

2 x 400g cans cannellini beans, drained, rinsed

1 cup (250ml) chicken stock

2 tbsp lemon juice

2 tbsp coarsely chopped oregano, plus extra 2–3 tbsp leaves

1 tsp finely grated lemon zest

2 tbsp red wine vinegar

700g pork fillet (pork tenderloin), diced into 3cm pieces

2 tbsp flat-leaf parsley

strips of lemon zest (or use 2 tsp grated zest)

salt and freshly ground black pepper

lemon wedges, to serve

1   Heat 1 tablespoon of the olive oil in a saucepan over a medium heat. Add the onion and thinly sliced garlic to the pan; cook, stirring, for 6 minutes or until tender. Add the wine, stirring to combine, then add the cannellini beans and stock. Bring to a simmer; cook, stirring occasionally, for 15 minutes or until thickened. Crush the beans with a fork; stir in the lemon juice and the 2 tablespoons chopped oregano. Season with salt and pepper to taste. Cover and set aside to keep warm.

2   Meanwhile, process the remaining olive oil, lemon zest, garlic halves, red wine vinegar, and extra 2½ tablespoons oregano until the mixture forms a paste; season with salt and pepper to taste. Combine the oregano mixture and the pork in a medium bowl; thread the pork onto skewers.

3   Preheat an oiled ridged cast-iron grill pan (or grill or barbecue) to a medium heat. Cook the skewers, turning occasionally, for 6 minutes or until cooked through. Serve accompanied by the crushed white beans sprinkled with the parsley and strips of lemon zest, with lemon wedges for squeezing over.

TIP

If cooking the pork skewers in a ridged cast-iron grill pan, you won't need to soak the bamboo skewers first. However, if you are barbecuing on a grill with a live flame, you will need to do this, to prevent them from scorching or burning while cooking. Place the bamboo skewers in a tall jug, fill with boiling water from the kettle, and soak for 5 minutes; drain.

Fast pizza

When everyone comes home hungry and in a rush, or unexpected guests arrive at the door and you need to whip up a meal, reach for one – or more! – of these pizza ideas as the perfect solution. Indeed, you can use them any time the yen for a pizza is calling.

Salami, ricotta, and kale

PREP TIME + COOK TIME **15 MINUTES** | SERVES **4**

Oil 2 baking or pizza trays; place in the oven, then preheat to 240°C (220°C fan/475°F/Gas 9). On floured baking parchment, roll two 250g ready-made dough balls into two 15cm x 30cm ovals. Transfer the bases on the parchment to the trays; spread with $1/3$ cup (80ml) pizza sauce (with herbs and garlic). Top with 150g shaved mild Danish or other salami, 500g cherry vine tomatoes, $1/2$ thinly sliced small red onion, and $1/2$ cup (130g) crumbled fresh ricotta; bake for 15 minutes or until the bases are browned and crisp. Serve topped with 60g baby kale leaves.

Teriyaki chicken and pineapple

PREP TIME + COOK TIME **15 MINUTES** | SERVES **4**

Oil 2 baking or pizza trays; place in the oven, then preheat to 240°C (220°C fan/475°F/Gas 9). On floured baking parchment, roll two 250g ready-made dough balls into two 15cm x 30cm ovals. Transfer the bases on the parchment to the trays. Drain a 227g can pineapple pieces; drain again on kitchen paper. Combine $1/3$ cup (80ml) barbecue sauce with 2 tablespoons teriyaki sauce in a small jug. Spread two-thirds of the sauce mixture onto the bases; top with $1^1/2$ cups (260g) shredded barbecued or chargrilled chicken, 1 thinly sliced small red pepper, 1 thinly sliced flat mushroom, and the drained pineapple. Bake the pizzas for 15 minutes or until the bases are browned and crisp. Serve drizzled with the remaining sauce mixture and sprinkled with 2 thinly sliced spring onions.

Tomato and mozzarella

PREP TIME + COOK TIME **15 MINUTES** | SERVES **4**

Oil 2 baking or pizza trays; place in the oven, then preheat to 240°C (220°C fan/475°F/Gas 9). On floured baking parchment, roll two 250g ready-made dough balls into two 15cm x 30cm ovals. Transfer the bases on the parchment to the trays; spread with $1/2$ cup (125ml) passata. Top with 400g thickly sliced mixed baby heirloom tomatoes and 150g torn buffalo mozzarella. Bake the pizzas for 15 minutes or until the bases are browned and crisp. Drizzle with 1 tablespoon olive oil and 2 teaspoons balsamic vinegar. Sprinkle with 1 tablespoon roasted pine nuts, $1/4$ cup (15g) small fresh basil leaves, and $1/4$ cup (25g) shaved Parmesan.

Sweet potato and rosemary

PREP TIME + COOK TIME **15 MINUTES** | SERVES **4**

Oil 2 oven or pizza trays; place in the oven, then preheat to 240°C (220°C fan/475°F/Gas 9). On floured baking parchment, roll two 250g ready-made dough balls into two 15cm x 30cm ovals. Transfer the bases on the paper to the trays; spread with combined $1/3$ cup (80ml) olive oil, 1 crushed garlic clove, and 1 tablespoon chopped rosemary. Using a vegetable peeler, mandolin, or V-slicer, slice 1 small orange sweet potato into paper-thin strips. Sprinkle with 100g crumbled feta. Bake the pizzas for 15 minutes or until the bases are browned and crisp. Serve topped with 50g rocket leaves and drizzled with 1 tablespoon olive oil.

Mushroom and goat's cheese ravioli with brown butter

MEAT-FREE | PREP + COOK TIME **30 MINUTES + STANDING & COOLING** | SERVES **4**

Gyoza wrappers are used to make this elegantly simple ravioli. The brown butter sauce is made by gently cooking butter to the point where the milk solids separate from the fat and are transformed into a toasty, sweet-flavoured mixture.

200g chestnut mushrooms

100g marinated goat's cheese (reserve the oil)

¼ cup (7g) tarragon leaves, plus extra, to serve

24 gyoza wrappers

75g butter

¼ cup (25g) walnuts, coarsely chopped, plus extra, to serve

salt and freshly ground black pepper

1 Finely chop the mushrooms. Heat 1 tablespoon of the goat's cheese marinating oil in a medium frying pan over a medium-high heat; cook the mushrooms, stirring, for 4 minutes or until soft. Season with salt and pepper to taste. Transfer to a heatproof bowl; allow to cool to room temperature. Reserve the frying pan, without rinsing.

2 Finely chop 2 tablespoons of the tarragon. Add the chopped tarragon and goat's cheese to the cooled mushroom mixture; stir to combine.

3 Place 12 gyoza wrappers on a clean work surface. Spoon the filling onto the centre of each wrapper. Dampen around the edge of each wrapper with a little water; top with the remaining wrappers, pressing together the edges to seal.

4 Cook the ravioli in a large saucepan of boiling salted water, in batches, for 2 minutes or until they float to the surface. Remove the ravioli with a slotted spoon; place in a single layer on a tray. Cover to keep warm.

5 Melt the butter in the reserved frying pan over a low heat. Add the walnuts and remaining tarragon leaves; cook gently until the butter begins to turn a nutty brown colour. Add the cooked ravioli to the pan; toss gently to coat. Remove the pan from the heat.

6 Serve the ravioli topped with extra tarragon leaves and extra walnuts. Season with pepper to taste.

TIP

If you can't find gyoza wrappers, you can use square wonton wrappers or other dumpling wrappers instead.

Steak and spuds with salsa verde

GLUTEN-FREE | PREP + COOK TIME **30 MINUTES** | SERVES **4**

Salsa verde, the ubiquitous Italian green sauce, livens up most things. Variations of salsa verde are found in Spanish and French cooking, too. If you have sauce left over, slather it in a roll to elevate a sandwich or drizzle over veggies to add a burst of flavour.

1½ tbsp extra virgin olive oil

500g small kipfler (fingerling) potatoes, halved lengthways

8 x 100g beef fillet medallions

1 bunch of watercress (350g), trimmed (see tip)

salt and freshly ground black pepper

salsa verde

1 garlic clove, crushed

1 tsp Dijon mustard

2 tsp baby capers

2 anchovy fillets

3 tsp red wine vinegar

3 cornichons

¼ cup (5g) mint leaves

¼ cup (7g) basil leaves

2 tbsp coarsely chopped flat-leaf parsley

¼ cup (60ml) extra virgin olive oil

1 Preheat the oven to 220°C (200°C fan/425°F/Gas 7).

2 Line a baking tray with baking parchment. Toss the potatoes with half of the olive oil on the tray; season with salt and pepper to taste. Roast the potatoes for 20 minutes or until golden and tender.

3 Heat the remaining olive oil over a medium-high heat in a large frying pan; cook the beef for 2½ minutes on each side for medium, or until cooked to your liking. Set aside to keep warm while making the sauce.

4 To make the salsa verde, process the ingredients until finely chopped; season with salt and pepper to taste.

5 Serve the steak with the potatoes, watercress, and salsa verde.

TIP

To prepare the watercress, pick off and use the smaller sprigs and discard the larger, thicker stems, which are more peppery.

Spanish chicken, chorizo, and rice soup

CHEAP EAT | PREP + COOK TIME **30 MINUTES** | SERVES **4**

Comfort in a bowl, this hearty dish is a soupier version of the classic Spanish chicken and rice. If you'd like to ramp up the flavours in the soup even further, swap the sweet paprika for Spanish smoked paprika and add a pinch of dried red chilli flakes.

30g butter

1 small onion (80g), finely chopped

2 garlic cloves, crushed

1 red pepper (200g), finely chopped

2 tsp dried oregano

1 tsp sweet paprika

1 tsp ground cumin

1 tbsp plain flour

2 tbsp tomato purée

4 cups (1 litre) chicken stock

400g can crushed tomatoes

1/2 cup (100g) uncooked white medium-grain rice

170g cured chorizo, thinly sliced

2 cups (320g) shredded cooked chicken

1 large avocado (320g)

1/2 cup (25g) coarsely chopped coriander

salt and freshly ground black pepper

2 limes, halved, to serve

1 Melt the butter in a large saucepan over a medium heat; cook the onion and garlic, stirring, for 5 minutes or until the onion softens. Add the red pepper, oregano, paprika, and ground cumin; cook, stirring, until fragrant. Add the flour and tomato purée; cook, stirring, for 1 minute. Gradually stir in the stock, 2 cups (500ml) water, and the crushed tomatoes; bring to the boil, stirring. Stir in the rice; simmer uncovered, stirring occasionally, for 15 minutes or until the rice is tender.

2 Meanwhile, heat a large oiled frying pan over a medium-high heat. Cook the chorizo until browned. Drain on kitchen paper.

3 Add the chorizo and chicken to the soup; stir over a medium heat until hot. Season with salt and pepper to taste. Finely chop the avocado.

4 Serve bowls of the soup topped with the avocado and coriander, and accompanied by the lime halves for squeezing over.

Veal scaloppine with lemon and capers

GLUTEN-FREE | PREP + COOK TIME **30 MINUTES** | SERVES **6**

Veal scaloppine, veal escalopes, veal schnitzel – all three are one and the same. Thinly sliced into steaks, they are available crumbed or plain (uncrumbed). We used plain in this recipe. You could serve the veal with mashed potato instead of polenta, if you like.

1 cup (170g) instant polenta

³/₄ cup (180ml) milk

¹/₄ cup (25g) finely grated Parmesan

1 tbsp cracked black pepper

6 thin veal escalopes (600g)

60g butter

1 tbsp drained baby capers, rinsed

3 strips of lemon zest, thinly sliced

¹/₃ cup (80ml) lemon juice

2 tbsp micro parsley

salt and freshly ground black pepper

1 Bring 2 cups (500ml) water to the boil in a medium saucepan. Stir in the polenta, and reduce the heat to low. Cook, stirring, for 5 minutes or until the polenta thickens. Stir in the milk; cook, still stirring, for 5 minutes or until the polenta thickens. Stir in the Parmesan; season with salt and pepper to taste. Keep warm until needed.

2 Meanwhile, sprinkle the 1 tablespoon cracked black pepper over both sides of the veal. Heat the butter in a large frying pan over a medium-high heat; cook the veal, in batches, for 2–3 minutes on each side or until lightly browned. Remove from the pan; cover and set aside to keep warm.

3 Add the capers, lemon zest, lemon juice, and 1 tablespoon water to the same pan; bring to the boil, stirring. Spoon the sauce over the veal, and sprinkle with the parsley. Serve the polenta with the veal.

TIP

Serve the veal with steamed green beans and sprinkle the polenta with extra grated Parmesan, if you like.

Couscous and dill crusted fish

HEALTHY CHOICE | PREP + COOK TIME **20 MINUTES** | SERVES **4**

This recipe showcases a clever way to use couscous, flavoured with fresh dill and garlic, as a crunchy coating on the fish. Oven-baking rather than pan-frying the fish takes it all one step further, to keep things healthy.

½ cup (100g) instant couscous

4 tbsp coarsely chopped dill

2 garlic cloves, crushed

2 tbsp extra virgin olive oil

4 x 200g skinless firm white fish fillets

175g broccolini (Tenderstem broccoli), thickly sliced on the diagonal

2 cups (240g) frozen garden peas

1 cup (280g) Greek-style yogurt

2 tbsp tahini

1 tbsp lemon juice

⅓ cup (25g) flaked almonds, toasted

salt and freshly ground black pepper

lemon wedges, to serve

1 Preheat the oven to 220°C (200°C fan/425°F/Gas 7). Line a large baking tray with baking parchment.

2 Put the couscous, 2 tablespoons of the chopped dill, half of the crushed garlic, ½ cup (125ml) water, and the olive oil in a small bowl. Using your fingertips, rub the couscous grains until evenly covered with the mixture; season with salt and pepper to taste. Place the fish on the prepared baking tray; press the couscous mixture onto the fish. Bake for 12 minutes or until the fish is cooked through and the crust is golden.

3 Meanwhile, cook the broccolini in a saucepan of boiling water for 2 minutes. Add the peas; cook for a further minute or until the vegetables are tender; drain.

4 Combine the yogurt, tahini, lemon juice, and remaining crushed garlic in a small bowl; season with salt and pepper to taste. Spoon the yogurt mixture onto 4 plates. Top with the vegetables, fish, almonds, and remaining 2 tablespoons chopped dill. Serve with the lemon wedges for squeezing over.

TIP

You could also try this recipe with skinless salmon fillets replacing the white fish fillets.

Prawns with risoni and peas

KID-FRIENDLY | PREP + COOK TIME **20 MINUTES** | SERVES **2**

Garlicky prawns and mushy peas combine here to make a light but satisfying meal perfect for summer evenings. You could make the recipe using vongole (clams) instead of prawns and moghrabieh (giant couscous) instead of risoni. The recipe can easily be doubled to serve four.

20g butter, chopped

2 garlic cloves, crushed

$1/2$ cup (125ml) chicken stock

$2^1/2$ cups (300g) frozen garden peas

1 cup (220g) dried risoni pasta

4 tbsp extra virgin olive oil

12 shelled uncooked medium prawns (540g), tails intact

$1/4$ cup (7g) coarsely chopped flat-leaf parsley

1 long red chilli, seeded, finely chopped

salt and freshly ground black pepper

lemon wedges, to serve

1 Heat the butter in a small saucepan over a low heat. Once foaming, add half of the garlic; cook, stirring, until lightly golden. Add the stock and $1/2$ cup (125ml) water. Bring to the boil, then reduce the heat slightly. Add the peas; cook, covered, for 3 minutes or until tender. Remove and reserve $1/2$ cup (60g) of the peas. Set aside.

2 Cook the risoni in a saucepan of boiling water until almost tender; drain.

3 Meanwhile, heat 2 tablespoons of the olive oil in a large frying pan over a high heat. Cook the prawns for 1 minute. Add the remaining garlic, then turn the prawns over. Cook for a further minute or until changed in colour and just cooked through.

4 Using a hand-held blender (or small food processor), coarsely purée the pea and stock mixture; stir in the reserved whole peas. Season with salt and pepper to taste. Add the purée mixture and risoni to the pan with the prawns; stir to combine. Cook for a further minute or until heated through. Stir in the parsley and chilli.

5 To serve, divide the mixture between 2 bowls. Drizzle with the remaining 2 tablespoons olive oil. Serve accompanied by the lemon wedges for squeezing over.

TIP

Risoni is a rice-shaped pasta, as its name implies. Also known as orzo, which means 'barley' in Italian, it is often used in soups such as minestrone.

Steamed fish with tahini yogurt

HEALTHY CHOICE | PREP + COOK TIME **25 MINUTES** | SERVES **4**

This delicious and healthy pairing of fish with tahini yogurt is a popular combination throughout the Middle East, and especially in Lebanon where it is a coastal speciality and usually features baked fish and pine nuts. Almonds are used here instead.

4 x 200g skinless firm white fish fillets

$1/3$ cup (80ml) lemon juice

4 small courgettes (360g), trimmed, sliced lengthways into ribbons

6 radishes (280g), trimmed, thinly sliced

1 tbsp tahini

$1/3$ cup (95g) Greek-style yogurt

$1/4$ cup (10g) finely chopped coriander, plus extra $1/4$ cup (7g) coriander leaves

$1/2$ cup (70g) roasted slivered almonds

$1/4$ tsp dried chilli flakes

$1/4$ cup (60ml) extra virgin olive oil

salt and freshly ground black pepper

1 Put the fish in a steamer lined with baking parchment. Place the steamer over a saucepan of simmering water. Cook, covered, for 8 minutes or until the fish is just cooked through.

2 Meanwhile, combine the lemon juice, courgettes, and radishes in a small bowl; allow to stand until the vegetables are pickled, or until needed.

3 Combine the tahini and yogurt in a small bowl; season with salt and pepper to taste. Combine the $1/4$ cup (7g) chopped coriander, almonds, chilli flakes, and half of the olive oil in another small bowl.

4 Carefully transfer the fish from the steamer to a plate. Cover each portion generously with the tahini yogurt mixture, then top with the coriander mixture.

5 Add the remaining olive oil to the bowl with the courgettes and radishes, season with salt and pepper to taste; toss to combine.

6 Serve the fish with the pickled vegetables, with the extra coriander leaves sprinkled over the top. Accompany with couscous or flatbread, if you like.

TIPS

- You could make the recipe using salmon, if you like.
- Try replacing the courgettes with a shaved bulb of baby fennel.
- Use a mandolin or V-slicer to thinly slice the radishes and courgettes.

Pork parmigiana bake

KID-FRIENDLY | PREP + COOK TIME **25 MINUTES** | SERVES **4**

This delectable dish of layered tastes and textures has echoes of the Italian-American comfort-food classic. It can be served as is, or accompany it with a salad – or even mashed potato and fresh crusty bread, to soak up the juices.

1 small aubergine (230g), thinly sliced lengthways

extra virgin olive oil cooking spray

4 prosciutto slices (60g)

2 tbsp olive oil

4 uncrumbed pork escalopes (400g)

4 bocconcini (mozzarella balls) (240g)

2 tbsp finely grated Parmesan

400g can cherry tomatoes

⅓ cup (7g) cress or baby basil leaves

salt and freshly ground black pepper

1 Preheat a grill plate (or ridged cast-iron grill pan or barbecue) to a high heat. Spray the aubergine on both sides with the cooking spray. Cook for 2 minutes on each side or until browned and tender. Set aside.

2 Meanwhile, preheat the grill to a high heat. Arrange the prosciutto on a baking tray lined with foil; place under the grill. Grill for 3 minutes or until the prosciutto is browned and crisp. Remove from the grill; cover and set aside to keep warm. Do not turn off the grill.

3 Meanwhile, heat 1 tablespoon of the olive oil in a shallow 2-litre (8-cup) flameproof baking dish over a medium-high heat on the hob. Season the pork with salt and pepper to taste; cook for 1 minute on each side or until almost cooked through; remove from the heat. Remove the pork from the dish. Set aside on a plate to keep warm.

4 Slice the bocconcini thinly. Add the tomatoes to the baking dish. Arrange the pork on top, then top the pork with the sliced aubergine, bocconcini, and Parmesan.

5 Place the baking dish under the hot grill; cook for 3 minutes or until the bocconcini melts and the pork is cooked through.

6 To serve, spoon the tomato over the pork stacks. Top with the prosciutto and cress. Drizzle with the remaining 1 tablespoon olive oil, and serve.

TIP

Put the baking dish as close to the preheated grill as possible.

DESSERTS

Choose from an array of treats to satisfy dessert cravings – from melting meringues to oozy puddings, fresh fruit sensations to new twists on classic favourites.

Sumac strawberry pavlovas

GLUTEN-FREE | PREP + COOK TIME **10 MINUTES + REFRIGERATION** | SERVES **4**

Sumac is a purple-red, astringent spice, ground from berries growing on shrubs that flourish in the wild around the Mediterranean. Here, the sumac adds a tart, lemony flavour that contrasts well with the sweetness of the meringue nests.

250g strawberries,
thinly sliced into rounds (see tips)

⅓ cup (55g) icing sugar, sifted

1 tbsp sumac

300ml whipping cream

1 tsp vanilla bean paste

4 gluten-free meringue nests (240g) (see tips)

1 Combine the strawberries, sifted icing sugar, and sumac in a small bowl. Cover; refrigerate for 30 minutes.

2 Just before serving, beat together the cream and vanilla in a small bowl using an electric mixer until firm peaks form. Spoon the cream equally among the meringue nests, then top with the sumac strawberries. Serve immediately.

TIPS

▪ Don't slice the strawberries too thinly, or they will fall apart during refrigeration.

▪ Premade plain meringues are a gluten-free product, but always check the label first, to make sure there are no hidden extras.

Lamington cream layer cake

KID-FRIENDLY | PREP + COOK TIME **30 MINUTES** | SERVES **8**

The lamington was originally created by a cook as a way of refreshing sponge cake. Debate swirls around what makes a 'proper' lamington, with some devotees firmly in the no-jam-or-cream camp, but all agree on the soaking of chocolate icing with a coconut coating.

300ml whipping cream

460g packaged double unfilled chocolate sponge cake rounds

1/2 cup (160g) strawberry jam

453g tub milk chocolate icing

1 1/2 cups (120g) shredded coconut

1 Using an electric mixer, beat the cream in a small bowl until firm peaks form.

2 Split the sponge cakes in half. Place a cake layer on a board; spread with 2 tablespoons of the jam. Top with one-third of the cream, leaving a 1cm border around the edge; top with another cake layer. Repeat the layering with the remaining jam, cream, and cake layers, finishing with a cake layer.

3 Spread the side of the cake with three-quarters of the chocolate icing. Place the coconut on a tray; shake slightly to form an even layer. Holding the top and bottom of the cake, roll the side of the cake in the coconut.

4 Spread the remaining icing over the top of the cake, then gently press the remaining coconut all over the top of the cake.

TIPS

- You can also make the lamington cake using vanilla sponge cakes and a tub of dark chocolate icing for a variation.
- If you can't find unfilled chocolate sponge rounds, you could use your favourite chocolate sponge recipe instead. Make the cake a day ahead, if you like, and put together on the day of eating.
- Alternatively, buy a chocolate cake with thin, soft icing such as chocolate mud cake (you may need 2 cakes). Slice as needed into 4 horizontal layers, then continue with the recipe.

Salted caramel and apple ice-cream sundaes

KID-FRIENDLY | PREP + COOK TIME **10 MINUTES** | SERVES **4**

These sundaes seem like autumnal decadence in a glass – but you can enjoy them at any time of the year. You could use pears instead of apples. Make sure to choose a firm variety of pear that holds its shape during cooking, such as Packham or Beurre Bosc.

80g butter, chopped

2 large apples (400g), peeled, coarsely chopped

1 tbsp lemon juice

$^1/_2$ cup (75g) light soft brown sugar

$^1/_4$ tsp mixed spice

$^1/_4$ tsp sea salt flakes

$^1/_4$ cup (60ml) whipping cream

8 scoops of good-quality vanilla ice cream

4 amaretti biscuits, crumbled

$^1/_4$ cup (40g) toasted pine nuts

1 Melt the butter in a large frying pan over a medium heat. Add the apples and lemon juice; cook for 5 minutes. Add the brown sugar, mixed spice, sea salt, and cream; cook, stirring, for 1 minute.

2 Divide the ice cream among 4 glasses. Spoon over the warm apple mixture; sprinkle with the crumbled biscuits and pine nuts. Serve the sundaes immediately.

TIP

To create more flavour variations of this recipe use a different-flavoured ice cream or nuts such as pecans or hazelnuts.

Fast ice-cream sandwiches

The only thing speedier than preparing these ice-cream sandwiches is how fast they will be devoured. Serve them for a children's party or for adults who are big kids themselves. They also work well for casual entertaining because they are the dessert equivalent of finger food.

Pretzel caramel

PREP TIME **20 MINUTES + FREEZING** | MAKES **4**

Place 4 milk chocolate digestive biscuits, chocolate-side down, on a board. Working with one at a time, top each biscuit with a scoop of salted caramel or toffee ice cream, then sandwich with another chocolate digestive biscuit, chocolate-side up. Place on a tray lined with cling film; freeze for 10 minutes. Place 1 cup of salted pretzels in a plastic zip-top bag; pound with a rolling pin until coarsely crushed. Place in a shallow bowl. Again working with one at a time, roll the sides of the ice-cream sandwiches in the crushed pretzels. Serve immediately or freeze until needed.

Fruity fizz

PREP TIME **20 MINUTES + FREEZING** | MAKES **4**

Place 4 pink iced biscuits, icing-side down, on a board. Working with one at a time, top each biscuit with a scoop of berry swirl ice cream, then sandwich with another pink iced biscuit, icing-side up. Place on a tray lined with cling film; freeze for 10 minutes. Place 1 x 35g packet fizzy or sherbet sweets in a plastic zip-top bag; pound with a rolling pin until coarsely crushed. Place in a shallow bowl. Again working with one at a time, roll the sides of the ice-cream sandwiches in the crushed sweets. Serve immediately or freeze until needed.

Loaded triple choc

PREP TIME **20 MINUTES + FREEZING** | MAKES **4**

Place 4 chocolate chip cookies, rounded-side down, on a board. Working with one at a time, top each cookie with a scoop of chocolate ice cream, then sandwich with another chocolate chip cookie, rounded-side up. Place on a tray lined with cling film; freeze for 10 minutes. Place ½ cup of mini M&Ms or Smarties in a shallow bowl. Again working with one at a time, roll the sides of the ice-cream sandwiches in the M&Ms. Serve immediately or freeze until needed.

Minty crisp

PREP TIME **20 MINUTES + FREEZING** | MAKES **4**

Place 4 peppermint patties or dark chocolate digestive biscuits, rounded-side down, on a board. Working with one at a time, top each biscuit with a scoop of mint choc chip ice cream, then sandwich with another peppermint pattie, rounded-side up. Place on a tray lined with cling film; freeze for 10 minutes. Finely chop 2 x 35g peppermint crisp or other peppermint chocolate bars; place in a shallow bowl. Again working with one at a time, roll the sides of the ice-cream sandwiches in the crushed peppermint crisp. Serve immediately or freeze until needed.

Charred peaches with berry rosewater yogurt

GLUTEN-FREE | PREP + COOK TIME **15 MINUTES** | SERVES **4**

Ripe, juicy stone fruits are often best treated simply, so that their sweet, subtle flavours become the stars of the show. For a nut-free version, replace the pistachios with toasted flaked coconut or pumpkin seeds, or omit them altogether; it will be equally delicious.

6 peaches (900g), halved, stones removed

2 tbsp coarsely chopped pistachios

berry rosewater yogurt

150g strawberries, sliced

1 tbsp rosewater

1 cup (280g) gluten-free vanilla yogurt

1 To make the berry rosewater yogurt, blend or process the strawberries with the rosewater until smooth. Swirl through the yogurt.

2 Preheat an oiled grill plate (or ridged cast-iron grill pan or barbecue) to a medium-high heat. Cook the peaches, cut-side down, for 5 minutes or until charred and tender.

3 Divide the peaches among 4 serving plates. Spoon the berry rosewater yogurt over the peaches. Serve with the chopped pistachios sprinkled over the top.

TIP

You can use thawed frozen strawberries or raspberries for this recipe, and either white or yellow peaches. If peaches are unavailable, mango cheeks, pineapple wedges, small ripe pear halves, or thick apple slices make good alternatives.

Waffles à la Suzette

KID-FRIENDLY | PREP + COOK TIME **20 MINUTES** | SERVES **4**

Traditionally Suzette sauce, a wonderful alchemy of caramelized sugar, butter, orange juice, and orange liqueur, accompanies crêpes. Waffles replace crêpes in our recipe to create an instant dessert, minus the flambée.

125g butter, chopped

$\frac{1}{2}$ cup (110g) caster sugar

2 tsp finely grated orange zest

$\frac{1}{2}$ cup (125ml) orange juice

8 Belgian-style waffles (480g)

2 oranges (480g), peeled, thinly sliced into rounds

2 cups (500ml) vanilla ice cream

2 tbsp toasted flaked almonds

1 To make the Suzette sauce, melt the butter in a small heavy-based saucepan. Add the caster sugar, orange zest, and orange juice; cook, stirring, over a low heat and without boiling, until the sugar dissolves. Bring to the boil. Reduce the heat; simmer, without stirring, for 2 minutes or until the sauce thickens slightly.

2 Warm the waffles according to the packet directions.

3 Divide the waffles and orange slices among 4 serving plates. Top with scoops of the ice cream, Suzette sauce, and a scattering of almonds.

TIP

If you would like to include orange liqueur, add 2 tablespoons in step 1 with the orange juice.

Pink lemonade fools

KID-FRIENDLY | PREP + COOK TIME **15 MINUTES + COOLING** | SERVES **4**

Fruit fools have a centuries-long history in British cooking, with the gooseberry fool being perhaps the most famous. The strawberry fools here are topped with Persian candyfloss (pashmak), with its fine filaments of pulled sugar; regular candyfloss may be substituted.

250g strawberries, hulled

1/3 cup (80ml) lemonade

300ml whipping cream

1/3 cup (110g) lemon curd

1/3 cup (15g) toasted coconut flakes, plus extra 1 tbsp

1 1/2 cups (6g) pink Persian candyfloss (pashmak)

1   Thinly slice 4 strawberries into rounds; quarter the remaining strawberries. Place the quartered strawberries and lemonade in a small frying pan over a high heat; bring to the boil. Reduce the heat; simmer for 5 minutes, mashing the strawberries with a fork a few times during cooking, or until the strawberries soften slightly and the liquid thickens slightly. Allow to cool.

2   Meanwhile, beat the cream in a small bowl using an electric mixer until soft peaks form. Fold the lemon curd and coconut flakes into the cream. Spoon three-quarters of the strawberry mixture onto the cream mixture; do not stir.

3   Spoon the cream mixture into four 2/3 cup (160ml) glasses. Top with the remaining strawberry mixture, reserved sliced strawberries, candy floss, and extra coconut.

TIP

You could also make the fools with other berries, such as blueberries or raspberries, if you like.

Peanut brittle cannoli

KID-FRIENDLY | PREP + COOK TIME **15 MINUTES** | SERVES **6**

Beloved Sicilian pastries, cannoli are one of those sweet treats where it's difficult to limit yourself to just one. For a more traditional filling, process 150g fresh ricotta until smooth. Whip ½ cup double cream to soft peaks; fold the cream and ricotta through the brittle.

300ml whipping cream

2 tsp vanilla extract

200g chocolate-coated peanut brittle, finely chopped

12 ready-made cannoli shells (150g)

sifted icing sugar, to dust

chocolate sauce

300ml whipping cream

100g dark chocolate (at least 70% cocoa), coarsely chopped

1 To make the chocolate sauce, heat the cream in a small saucepan until almost boiling, being careful not to scorch; remove from the heat. Add the chocolate; whisk until smooth.

2 Beat together the cream and vanilla in a small bowl using an electric mixer until firm peaks form; stir in 150g of the peanut brittle.

3 Fit a large piping bag with a large plain nozzle; fill with the peanut brittle cream. Pipe the filling into the cannoli shells; dust with the sifted icing sugar. Serve the cannoli with the chocolate sauce and remaining brittle.

TIPS

• Peanut brittle is available from major supermarkets and confectionery stores.
• If you don't have a piping bag, simply use a zip-top bag; fill the bag with the cream mixture, twist, and snip a 1cm hole from one corner.
• If you can't find cannoli shells, you could use brandy snap shells instead.

Banana pancakes with chocolate sauce

KID-FRIENDLY | PREP + COOK TIME **30 MINUTES** | SERVES **4**

Bananas and chocolate: a match made in heaven – for chocolate lovers at least. But if bananas aren't your thing in this part of the equation, you can swap them out for another fruit by using the same weight of fresh or frozen blueberries or raspberries instead.

1 cup (150g) self-raising flour

2 tbsp caster sugar

1¼ cups (310ml) buttermilk

1 egg, lightly beaten

2 tsp pure maple syrup

20g butter, melted and cooled

1 banana (200g), thinly sliced

½ cup (125ml) whipping cream

2 x 60g Snickers or other chocolate-covered caramel peanut bars, coarsely chopped

2 cups (500ml) chocolate ice cream

1 Sift the flour into a large bowl; stir in the sugar. Whisk in the combined buttermilk, egg, maple syrup, and butter until the batter is smooth. Stir in the banana.

2 Heat a large oiled frying pan over a medium heat. Pour ¼ cup of the batter into the pan, allowing room for spreading. (You should be able to fit more than 1 pancake in the pan at a time.) Cook for 2 minutes or until bubbles appear on the surface of the pancakes. Turn the pancakes over; cook for 2 minutes or until browned. Remove from the pan; cover to keep warm. Repeat with the remaining batter to make a total of 8 pancakes.

3 Meanwhile, heat the cream in a small saucepan over a low heat, add the Snickers bars; stir until melted.

4 Serve the banana pancakes topped with scoops of the chocolate ice cream and the choc-peanut sauce.

Lemon and meringue passionfruit mess

GLUTEN-FREE | PREP + COOK TIME **15 MINUTES** | SERVES **8**

Here, lemon curd and passionfruit pulp replace the usual strawberries found in Eton mess, and yogurt is added to the usual cream. It is still a quintessentially summer dessert, though, with its crisp meringue and soft, plump raspberries capping it all off.

300ml whipping cream

2 tbsp icing sugar

1 cup (280g) Greek-style yogurt

8 gluten-free meringue nests (80g), coarsely crushed

²⁄₃ cup (200ml) gluten-free lemon curd

¹⁄₃ cup (80g) passionfruit pulp (you will need 4–5 passionfruit)

¹⁄₃ cup (15g) flaked coconut, toasted

125g fresh raspberries

1 Using an electric mixer, beat together the cream and icing sugar in a small bowl until firm peaks form; gently fold in the yogurt.

2 Arrange half of the meringue pieces over a platter. Spoon the cream mixture over the meringue; drop spoonfuls of the lemon curd over the cream. Using a small knife, swirl the curd through the cream.

3 Top with the remaining crumbled meringue, passionfruit pulp, flaked coconut, and raspberries.

Microwave choc-orange self-saucing pudding

ONE-POT/KID-FRIENDLY | PREP + COOK TIME **25 MINUTES** | SERVES **4**

It may seem a paradox, but self-saucing puddings work by pouring a more liquidy mixture over a denser batter. During cooking, the liquid falls through the batter as it cooks, to produce an oozing sauce on the bottom of the pudding.

60g butter, chopped

³/₄ cup (110g) self-raising flour, sifted

¹/₃ cup (110g) caster sugar

2 tbsp cocoa powder, plus extra 2 tsp

²/₃ cup (160ml) milk

¹/₂ tsp vanilla extract

2 x 38g orange chocolate bars, coarsely chopped

¹/₄ cup (55g) firmly packed light soft brown sugar

1 cup (250ml) boiling water

1   Put 30g of the chopped butter in a deep 1.5-litre (6-cup) microwave-safe dish. Melt in a microwave oven on HIGH (100%) for 1 minute.

2   Add the sifted flour, caster sugar, and the 2 tablespoons cocoa powder to the dish with the milk and vanilla extract; whisk until smooth. Stir in the orange chocolate.

3   Combine the brown sugar and sifted extra 2 teaspoons cocoa powder in a medium jug; gradually stir in the boiling water. Add the remaining 30g chopped butter; stir until the butter melts. Carefully pour the syrup mixture evenly over the back of a spoon, over the pudding mixture.

4   Microwave on HIGH (100%) for 10 minutes or until just cooked in the centre. Allow to stand for 5 minutes before serving with cream or ice cream.

TIP

Don't wait too long to serve the pudding, or all the sauce will soak into the pudding before you have a chance to enjoy it.

Coconut rice with mango and raspberries

GLUTEN-FREE | PREP + COOK TIME **15 MINUTES** | SERVES **4**

This is a delectable summery rendition of rice pudding, served cool and with the tropical notes of coconut and mango singing through the creamy rice. The tart raspberries cut through the sweetness of the mango and provide acidic balance.

300ml whipping cream

$^1/_2$ cup (125ml) coconut cream

$^1/_2$ cup (80g) icing sugar

2$^1/_4$ cups (340g) cooked medium-grain white rice

1 large mango (600g), thinly sliced

125g raspberries

$^1/_2$ cup (25g) toasted flaked coconut

1 Beat the cream, coconut cream, and sugar in a small bowl with an electric mixer until soft peaks form.

2 Place the rice in a large bowl; fold in the cream mixture. Cover with cling film; refrigerate while preparing the mango.

3 Blend or process the mango until smooth. Divide the rice mixture and mango purée, in alternate layers, among four 1-cup (250ml) serving glasses; top with the raspberries and coconut.

TIPS

- Substitute papaya or summer berries for the mango, if you like.
- If you would like to cook your own rice, you will need about $^3/_4$ cup uncooked medium-grain white rice for this recipe.

Grilled pineapple with mint syrup

GLUTEN-FREE | PREP + COOK TIME **30 MINUTES** | SERVES **8**

Perfectly simple and perfectly delicious, pineapple takes on an intense sweetness when grilled. Choose a yellow-fleshed pineapple for the best flavour. You could use mango cheeks cut from 4 mangoes instead of the pineapple. Drizzle with passionfruit pulp, if you like.

^{1}/$_2$ cup (110g) caster sugar

1^1/$_2$ cups (40g) firmly packed mint leaves, plus extra ^{1}/$_4$ cup (5g), to serve

1 cup (50g) coconut flakes

1 yellow-fleshed pineapple (1.25kg), cut crossways into 1.5cm thick slices

1 litre (4 cups) vanilla or passionfruit frozen yogurt

1 Preheat the oven to 180°C (160°C fan/350°F/Gas 4).

2 Stir the caster sugar and ^{1}/$_2$ cup (125ml) water in a small saucepan, over a medium heat, for 4 minutes or until the sugar dissolves and the syrup reduces slightly. Transfer to a small stainless-steel bowl; freeze for 15 minutes to chill rapidly.

3 Meanwhile, put the 1^1/$_2$ cups (40g) mint in a heatproof bowl. Cover with boiling water; allow to stand for 10 seconds. Drain, then refresh under cold running water. Squeeze to remove any excess water. Set aside.

4 Place the coconut on a baking tray; bake, shaking the tray occasionally, for 3 minutes or until golden. Set aside.

5 Preheat a large grill plate (or ridged cast-iron grill pan or barbecue) to a medium-high heat. Cook the pineapple, in two batches, for 2 minutes on each side or until golden.

6 Process the blanched mint and cooled sugar syrup until finely chopped.

7 Divide the grilled pineapple among 8 plates; top with the frozen yogurt. Drizzle with the mint syrup. Serve sprinkled with the toasted coconut and the extra ^{1}/$_4$ cup (5g) mint leaves.

Cherry hazelnut cake

ONE-POT | PREP + COOK TIME **30 MINUTES + STANDING** | SERVES **8**

Make sure to warn eaters that the cherries contain pips. If you like, you could add 1 teaspoon of either finely grated lemon zest or finely grated orange zest when beating the butter and sugar in step 2. Ground almonds can also be used in place of ground hazelnuts.

150g butter, softened, plus extra for greasing

²/₃ cup (150g) caster sugar

2 eggs

½ cup (75g) plain flour

1½ cups (180g) ground hazelnuts

16 fresh cherries (150g), stalks attached

sifted icing sugar, to dust

¾ cup (180ml) double cream

⅓ cup (80ml) maple syrup

1 Preheat the oven to 200°C (180°C fan/400°F/Gas 6). Grease a 19cm square cake tin; line the bottom and sides with baking parchment, extending the parchment 5cm above the edges.

2 Using an electric mixer, beat together the butter and sugar in a small bowl until pale and fluffy. Add the eggs. Beat until just combined, then add the sifted flour and hazelnuts. Continue beating on low speed until just combined.

3 Spread the mixture evenly into the prepared cake tin; bake for 10 minutes.

4 Top the cake with the cherries, gently pushing them a quarter of the way into the mixture. Bake the cake for a further 10 minutes or until a skewer inserted into the centre comes out clean. Stand the cake in the tin for 3 minutes before turning, top-side up, onto a board. Dust with sifted icing sugar. Serve the cake warm, with dollops of the cream and maple syrup drizzled over the top.

Warm rhubarb and ginger coconut trifles

KID-FRIENDLY | PREP + COOK TIME **25 MINUTES** | SERVES **4**

Take advantage of the rhubarb season to make these pretty ruby trifles. Select rhubarb with the reddest stems for the best taste and look, and choose good-quality custard and flavourful cake. Using the best of what's available is key when there are so few elements in a dish.

3¼ cups (400g) coarsely chopped rhubarb stems (see tips)

2 tbsp orange juice

¼ cup (55g) caster sugar

2 cups (500ml) thick vanilla custard

250g ginger cake, chopped (see tips)

⅓ cup (20g) toasted flaked coconut

2 tbsp coarsely chopped pistachios

1 Combine the rhubarb, orange juice, and caster sugar in a medium saucepan; bring to the boil. Reduce the heat; simmer, stirring occasionally, for 3 minutes or until the rhubarb is tender.

2 Meanwhile, heat the custard in a small saucepan over a low heat.

3 Divide the ginger cake among 4 heatproof serving glasses. Top with the warm custard, then the rhubarb mixture, flaked coconut, and pistachios. Serve immediately.

TIPS

▪ You need about 5 trimmed stems of rhubarb for this recipe.

▪ We used a bought ginger loaf cake for this recipe, available in the bakery section of most large supermarkets. If you can't find it you could use broken gingerbread biscuits instead.

Passionfruit, lemon, and coconut tarts

GLUTEN-FREE | PREP + COOK TIME **30 MINUTES + COOLING** | MAKES **12**

The cases for these tarts are ingeniously simple to make and a coconut delight to eat.
If passionfruit isn't available, you can top the coconut tarts with thinly sliced mango
or raspberries. They all work well with the tangy lemon curd.

a little butter for greasing

1 cup (90g) desiccated coconut

1 egg white, lightly beaten

2 tbsp caster sugar

2 tbsp whipping cream

1/2 cup (160g) gluten-free lemon curd

2 tbsp passionfruit pulp

1 Preheat the oven to 150°C (130°C fan/300°F/Gas 2). Grease a 12-hole (2-tbsp/40ml) mini muffin tin.

2 Combine the coconut, egg white, and sugar in a medium bowl. Press the mixture firmly and evenly over the bottoms and sides of the tin holes. Bake the coconut cases for 20 minutes or until lightly browned. Allow to cool; remove from the pan.

3 Meanwhile, beat the cream in a small bowl using an electric mixer until soft peaks form. Gently fold the lemon curd into the cream.

4 Divide the lemon mixture among the coconut cases. Top each tart with a little of the passionfruit pulp.

Dutch baby chocolate pancake with banana

KID-FRIENDLY | PREP + COOK TIME **25 MINUTES** | SERVES **4**

This triple-chocolate dessert is a breeze to make. Just make sure everyone knows that it's meant to be shared! Dutch baby pancakes are made as single large pancakes and baked in the oven, and the Dutch-process cocoa used here is mellower and darker than natural cocoa.

³/₄ cup (180ml) milk

²/₃ cup (100g) plain flour

4 eggs

2 tbsp Dutch-process cocoa powder, plus extra 1 tsp, sifted

½ cup (110g) caster sugar

1 tsp vanilla bean paste

100g dark chocolate (at least 70% cocoa), coarsely chopped

30g butter

2 small bananas (260g), halved lengthways and crossways

4 scoops of chocolate or chocolate chip ice cream

1   Preheat the oven to 200°C (180°C fan/400°F/Gas 6).

2   Pulse the milk, flour, eggs, the 2 tablespoons cocoa powder, caster sugar, vanilla bean paste, and a pinch of salt in a food processor for 15 seconds or until just combined (do not overprocess or the mixture will be tough). Stir in half of the chopped chocolate.

3   Heat the butter in an ovenproof frying pan with an 18cm base and 25cm top diameter, over a medium heat, for 1 minute or until foaming. Add the pancake batter. Immediately transfer to the oven; bake for 12 minutes or until puffed and cooked through.

4   Gently melt the remaining chocolate in a microwave or a small heatproof bowl over a saucepan of simmering water.

5   Top the pancake with the bananas and ice cream, drizzle with the melted chocolate, and dust with the extra 2 teaspoons sifted cocoa powder. Serve the pancake immediately.

TIP

Dutch-process cocoa powder is darker than natural cocoa powder and has a mellower flavour. It goes through an alkalizing process when it is made, neutralizing the natural acidity of the cocoa beans.

Spiced rhubarb and strawberry crumbles

KID-FRIENDLY | PREP + COOK TIME **25 MINUTES + COOLING** | SERVES **4**

Fruit crumbles are often seen as a comfort food for a wintry night, but this one makes the most of summer's seasonal bounty. The crumble mixture can be made a day ahead; store in an airtight container until needed. You can also serve it as a topping for other desserts.

a little butter for greasing

$1/4$ cup (60ml) maple syrup

100g shortbread, coarsely chopped (see tip)

110g macadamia halves

1 bunch of rhubarb (400g), trimmed (any leaves discarded), cut into 4cm pieces

250g strawberries, quartered

1 tsp vanilla extract

$1/4$ cup (55g) caster sugar

1 tsp ground ginger

$1/2$ tsp ground cinnamon

1 Preheat the oven to 200°C (180°C fan/400°F/Gas 6). Grease and line a baking tray with baking parchment.

2 Combine the maple syrup, shortbread, and macadamias in a medium bowl; spread out on the prepared baking tray. Bake in the oven for 4 minutes; stir, then bake for a further 4 minutes or until golden. Allow to cool.

3 Meanwhile, put the rhubarb, strawberries, vanilla extract, sugar, and spices in a medium saucepan over a medium heat; cook, stirring, for 3 minutes or until the juices run from the fruit. Continue cooking, stirring occasionally, for a further 5 minutes or until the rhubarb has softened but still holds its shape.

4 Divide the fruit mixture among 4 small bowls; top with the crumble mixture to serve.

TIP

You could also make the crumble mixture with your favourite biscuits; however, bear in mind that it is best to choose a buttery, un-iced variety.

Watermelon, lime, and berry cheesecake jars

KID-FRIENDLY | PREP + COOK TIME **15 MINUTES** | SERVES **4**

This superfast deconstructed cheesecake can be assembled and served in glasses or serving bowls instead of jars, if you like. Delving with your spoon through the layers of summer fruit and creamy cheese to find the gingery crumbs below becomes part of the joy of eating.

200g gingernut biscuits

50g butter, roughly chopped

1 lime (90g)

250g mascarpone

250g cream cheese

$^1/_3$ cup (55g) icing sugar, sifted, plus extra 2 tsp

125g raspberries

125g seedless watermelon, diced into 1cm pieces

1 tbsp finely shredded mint

1 Pulse the biscuits in a food processor until finely chopped. Add the butter; pulse until just combined. Divide the crumb mixture evenly among four 1½-cup (375ml) jars.

2 Finely grate the zest of the lime, then juice (you will need 2 tablespoons of lime juice). Process the lime zest and juice, mascarpone, cream cheese, and sifted icing sugar until smooth. Divide the cheese mixture evenly among the jars; tap gently on a work surface to level the mixture.

3 Put the raspberries and extra 2 teaspoons icing sugar in a bowl. Using the back of a fork, lightly crush the berries, stirring until the icing sugar dissolves. Stir in the watermelon.

4 Divide the watermelon mixture evenly among the jars; top each one with the mint to serve.

Chocolate dulce de leche puddings

KID-FRIENDLY | PREP + COOK TIME **30 MINUTES** | SERVES **4**

Dulce de leche is a Latin American caramel made by reducing milk and sugar until it is a gloriously thick, dark caramel. It can be used as a spread or topping for everything from cakes to ice cream, and has infinite uses in desserts.

$^{1}/_{3}$ cup (120g) dulce de leche

$^{3}/_{4}$ cup (165g) caster sugar

100g butter, melted, cooled, plus extra for greasing

$^{1}/_{3}$ cup (100g) self-raising flour, sifted

2 tbsp ground almonds

$^{1}/_{3}$ cup (35g) Dutch-process cocoa powder, sifted, plus extra $^{1}/_{2}$ tsp, to dust

$^{1}/_{3}$ cup (80ml) milk

2 eggs

1 tsp vanilla extract

50g dark chocolate (at least 70% cocoa), finely chopped

$^{1}/_{2}$ cup (110g) firmly packed light soft brown sugar

1 cup (250ml) boiling water

4 small scoops of vanilla ice cream

1 Preheat the oven to 200°C (180°C fan/400°F/Gas 6). Grease four 1$^{1}/_{3}$-cup (330ml) ovenproof dishes with a little butter; place on a baking tray lined with baking parchment.

2 Meanwhile, spoon 1 tablespoon of the dulce de leche into the bottom of each dish.

3 Process the caster sugar, melted butter, sifted flour, ground almonds, 2 tablespoons of the sifted cocoa powder, milk, eggs, and vanilla extract until smooth. Transfer the mixture to a large bowl; stir in the chopped chocolate. Spoon the mixture evenly into the prepared dishes.

4 Combine the brown sugar and remaining cocoa powder into a small bowl; sprinkle the sugar mixture evenly over puddings. Pour the boiling water into a small jug. Holding a spoon with the back facing upwards over each pudding, carefully pour $^{1}/_{4}$ cup boiling water over the surface of each pudding to wet the sugar mixture completely.

5 Bake the puddings for 25 minutes or until the top is cake-like and firm to the touch. Dust with the extra $^{1}/_{2}$ teaspoon sifted cocoa powder. Serve immediately, topped with the ice cream and accompanied by extra dulce de leche, if you like.

TIP

Dulce de leche is available in jars from delis and some supermarkets. Substitute with Carnation caramel dessert filling, if you can't find it.

Conversion chart

A note on Australian measures

- One Australian metric measuring cup holds approximately 250ml.

- One Australian metric tablespoon holds 20ml.

- One Australian metric teaspoon holds 5ml.

- The difference between one country's measuring cups and another's is within a two- or three-teaspoon variance, and should not affect your cooking results.

- North America, New Zealand, and the United Kingdom use a 15ml tablespoon.

Using measures in this book

- All cup and spoon measurements are level.

- The most accurate way of measuring dry ingredients is to weigh them.

- When measuring liquids, use a clear glass or plastic jug with metric markings.

- We use large eggs with an average weight of 60g. All fruit and vegetables are assumed to be medium unless otherwise stated.

Dry measures

metric	imperial
15g	$^1/_2$oz
30g	1oz
60g	2oz
90g	3oz
125g	4oz ($^1/_4$lb)
155g	5oz
185g	6oz
220g	7oz
250g	8oz ($^1/_2$lb)
280g	9oz
315g	10oz
345g	11oz
375g	12oz ($^3/_4$lb)
410g	13oz
440g	14oz
470g	15oz
500g	16oz (1lb)
750g	24oz (1$^1/_2$lb)
1kg	32oz (2lb)

Liquid measures

metric	imperial
30ml	1 fluid oz
60ml	2 fluid oz
100ml	3 fluid oz
125ml	4 fluid oz
150ml	5 fluid oz
190ml	6 fluid oz
250ml	8 fluid oz
300ml	10 fluid oz
500ml	16 fluid oz
600ml	20 fluid oz
1000ml (1 litre)	1$^3/_4$ pints

Length measures

metric	imperial
3mm	$^1/_8$in
6mm	$^1/_4$in
1cm	$^1/_2$in
2cm	$^3/_4$in
2.5cm	1in
5cm	2in
6cm	2$^1/_2$in
8cm	3in
10cm	4in
13cm	5in
15cm	6in
18cm	7in
20cm	8in
22cm	9in
25cm	10in
28cm	11in
30cm	12in (1ft)

Oven temperatures

The oven temperatures in this book are for conventional ovens; if you have a fan-forced oven, decrease the temperature by 10–20 degrees.

	°C (Celsius)	°F (Fahrenheit)
Very slow	120	250
Slow	150	300
Moderately slow	160	325
Moderate	180	350
Moderately hot	200	400
Hot	220	425
Very hot	240	475

Index

Acknowledgments

DK would like to thank Sophia Young, Joe Reville, Amanda Chebatte, and Georgia Moore for their assistance in making this book.

The Australian Women's Weekly Test Kitchen in Sydney has developed, tested, and photographed the recipes in this book.